How To Write Fiction For Cash

Laverne Ross

QC Quality of Course Inc

38 McArthur Ave
Ottawa On
K1L 6R2

CCIP

Ross, Laverne
How to Write Fiction for Cash

Includes index.
ISBN 1-895492-14-9

1. Fiction—Authorship. I. Title.

PN3355.R68 1994 808.3 C94-900368-9

Contents

PART ONE

INTRODUCTION

Writing fiction lets you share your life with people you create. They cry with you when you're sad, put up with your temperament without protest, and laugh at all the right times. They accompany you as you explore jungles, climb mountains, or frantically flee the dastardly denizens of life. Fiction is a wonderful escape and a journey of self-discovery.

Fiction can be divided into two parts: personal experience and convention. Personal experience is obvious. It is all those things that happened to you in your lifetime; those things waiting to be turned into a story.

Convention is the pattern of storytelling. It is "the technique, style, structure or subject-matter that is commonly used in literary works, by customary agreement or precedent rather than by natural necessity." (Oxford Dictionary of Literary Terms)

Conventions are essential to fiction and include narrative techniques such as the surprise ending, presentation and point of view, and archetypical characters. Fiction that relies almost entirely on personal experience, without regard for convention, tends to become muddled. On the other hand, when the use of convention is excessive, rigid and without elaboration, it becomes what is commonly called formula fiction.

Writing fiction is different from writing nonfiction. Fiction requires no research unless you are setting your story in a specific place. You do not have to conduct interviews or concern yourself with libel and invasion of privacy suits. Usually, you do not have to send a query letter to an editor unless you are writing a novel.

Fiction is harder to sell than nonfiction. It is imagination driven, limitless in its scope and, subject to the personal preferences of editors. However, editors are always looking for new talent so if you have a good idea and can present it in a gripping manner, you'll find a market for your work.

Novice writers tend to begin with fiction because they think it is easier. Not so. To write fiction you require a special kind of talent. You need to rely on your inventiveness to create situations that carry your characters excitingly from place to place. Everything must come alive for your reader.

Nonfiction finds reader interest in fact. You are "retelling" an event so imagination doesn't often enter into the construction. Successful nonfiction writers sometimes turn their hand to fiction but not all prevail.

If you are a fiction writer, you are always "writing" no matter what is going on in your life. People you meet become potential characters, places you visit become future locations, and conversations are mentally filed, then called upon to give a character depth.

One of the most frequently asked questions is What makes a fiction writer? The answer is standard: A natural aptitude for story telling, a lifelong habit of reading, love of language.

A fiction writer must possess an active imagination. Imagination cannot be created but it can be nurtured. It needs to be used, played with, listened to. It must be turned over and over so that all facets are explored and expanded. Only then can the most marvellous things find their way to paper.

The second attribute necessary for writing fiction is empathy. Empathy is defined as "the power to project one's personality into (and so fully comprehending) an object of contemplation." It differs from sympathy ("being simultaneously affected with the same feeling as another") in that the awareness usually comes from firsthand experience.

A person can feel sympathy for a mother who has lost a child but he cannot feel empathy unless he has experienced a similar loss.

Fiction writers write from inside other people as well as from inside themselves. It is this gift that produces strong and believable characters. Imagination can create the background, the scene, the dialogue, but empathy creates the real character and leads the reader through the recesses of that character's mind.

A writer of fiction must also possess style. Simply, it is the way in which a thing is said. If three people tell the same story, each will tell it in a different style. The best style produces the best story.

Every writer develops his own style and it should grow and change as he grows. Clear thinking manifests itself in clear writing and good style. Saying what you have to say, in words that make the reader see what you are seeing, is vital to style.

Your style is what distinguishes you from every other writer. Trying to copy a writer you admire only results in "second best" and commonly produces a great amount of frustration. Read . . . and read . . . and read. Learn what makes a particular writer's work successful, then set out to find your own voice.

Be yourself. Let the reader know who you are, what you are, and what you think. This does not mean you should preach your beliefs. It means be natural and honest with your feelings.

You need patience to become a good fiction writer. It takes time to develop the eye that sees a story or the ear that hears dialogue. But, patience isn't that simple. It goes beyond the struggle for perception.

On rare occasions, you will find yourself writing effortlessly. The words flow, the images come alive faster than you can put the words on paper. Your muse is giving you dictation!

Most of the time you patiently sit at the keyboard, dragging out words that seem to be little more than adequate. The first draft gives you the bones of the story, characters that seem like rags upon a stick, and locations that lack imagery. The second draft is better. The third, maybe even the fifth or sixth, finally gives you the finished product. You had the patience to stay with it.

Occasionally, words refuse to come at all. You are drowning in a sea of frustration. You are facing what is commonly referred to as Writer's Block. I don't believe there is such a thing but I do believe there is exhaustion!

When words refuse to come, take a break. Do something entirely away from the creative process. Physical work often refreshes the mind. You can't force good writing. You must have patience. We live in an age of instant gratification but you won't get it in writing. Your fulfilment comes from the pleasure of creating the work itself.

You must be determined. Many parts of the writing process can be learned and, with determination, practice and talent, you will find the success you seek. Never accept the level at which you are writing as the final plateau. It is imperative that you write and keep on writing, learning and improving as you go.

To be successful, you must be serious about your work. If you refuse to commit your mind and heart, your work will reflect it. Give everything you do the best you have to offer, and you will likely produce something worth reading.

It is up to you to find your weaknesses and correct them before an editor sees the manuscript. Learn from every criticism you get and fight the overwhelming desire to defend your mistakes. Unless you are open to tough assessment, constantly strive to improve your craft, and never forget you are a professional, you probably won't make it.

The last point is the most important. Do you really want to do this? There is a price to pay for the writer's life. You are isolated hour after hour, day after day, year after year. There are times when you'd rather be golfing or spending a day in the garden, but you have a deadline and it must be met.

There are times when the frustration of rejection makes you scream: Why am I doing this? If you are truly a writer, the answer comes back before the thought is formed: Because I want to!

There are easier ways to make a living than writing, but there are few vocations that are as rewarding—intellectually and spiritually.

YOUR WRITING ENVIRONMENT

The environment you create becomes an important part of your life. You need only think of the time you'll spend in the room to understand that you have to want to be there. This is no place for colours you dislike or spaces so cluttered a page is lost forever if it slips from your desk.

Obviously, you are going to buy for your office those things that are the most necessary, adding the rest later as funds allow. You know you need something to write on. Today, that is a computer. If you can't afford one, start saving and buy when you can. Every day the number of editors asking for electronic submission, and submission by hard copy and disk, increases.

When selecting a computer, buy only what you need and keep costs down. Remember, you are using the computer for writing so you need a good word processing programme . . . and not much else. Select the best you can afford, in the environment you find most comfortable, and be sure you have enough memory to add options later, if you wish.

The same can be said when you're considering the printer. If a laser is within your budget, then buy it. If not, get the best you can afford. Editors who must struggle through poor copy are apt to reject your manuscript without reading it.

A fax machine is becoming increasingly necessary. Not only does it save time, it saves money. Fax transmissions are immediate and queries seem to be answered when they are received. Submitting copy by fax must be cleared with the individual editors.

Computers have internal fax capabilities and the programmes are improving. Care must be taken if you decide this is the way you want to go because the modem must be compatible with your existing software. Also, you cannot transmit anything that is not generated by the computer. A fax modem and separate fax machine give you the best of both worlds.

Your office will need file space (detailed later), a telephone, a comfortable chair, a desk, and book shelves. Try to set up so that you have good natural light as well as artificial light. You are going to be using your eyes hours at a time so protect them.

The ambience you create will influence your writing. If you are relaxed, comfortable and contented, you will produce good quality work. If the colours make you edgy and you are fighting bad light, your work will reflect your feelings.

Add to your equipment only when you know you require it. You don't need a scanner just because it is today's "in" piece of technology. Your income is going to be erratic so buy wisely.

This book is going to take you through the various fiction markets. It will teach you what they are, show you how to write for them, and make suggestions for selling your work.

We are going to approach writing as a business with a reasonable expectation of profit. You are going to take writing from a hobby to a profession.

You will learn where to find your ideas and how to put them into words. Markets will open to you because you will understand the correct ways to submit your work. You'll write query letters the editors will read and you will learn how to write a full proposal, and when to use them.

You are going to say with pride, "I am a writer." I hope you are going to enjoy the process.

CHAPTER ONE

FINDING IDEAS

Ideas are not physical objects. You can't go shopping for them like you can for apples and oranges. To make things even more difficult, ideas cannot be created. You cannot create anything. You can only rearrange.

What you have to work with is your own experience and memory. You rearrange what you know and feel into the fictional pieces you share with others. Good stories are based on recalled emotion and experience. The strength or weakness of the idea determines the success or failure of the written piece.

There are several reasons why novice writers find it difficult to write from personal experience. They are afraid they will offend someone if they retell an incident from the past. They don't want to risk embarrassing people they know.

Some new writers are plagued with having too much humility. They feel they have nothing to say that will interest a reader. We all know a person who dominates the dinner party, telling tales of his escapades. Why should the written word be less boring?

Then there is the problem of staying true to a memory. Try writing about a deceased relative or friend. A decidedly eerie feeling surrounds you—they seem to be reading over your shoulder. Basing a character on someone still living can be even worse.

The writer's view of the past is much more subjective than you might think. The key to overcoming the stumbling blocks is to remember you are writing fiction. You are not presenting an account of a person's life. The character is not a mirror image of a real person's strengths and weaknesses.

The narrative is fantasy and you are free to express yourself any way you want.

Writers become adept in disguising the people, places, and incidents that are the models for their stories. They shift the location. They alter physical characteristics and change personality traits. They never use real names.

Our ideas of people are formed by our relationships with them. Fortunately, everyone doesn't see things the same way. Using a person you dislike as the character model for your villain usually produces an unrecognizable caricature. Your view will be slanted, the retelling of an incident, biased.

One word of caution. You must not reveal an identity, or present views of people as objective truth, or you will leave yourself open to a libel suit. Such cases are rare in fiction but they can happen.

There are times when a writer needs a trigger to jog a memory or bring an experience into focus. We call this the search for ideas. Ideas are all around you but they are of little use unless you can identify them.

1. PERSONAL EXPERIENCE

Everything around you has the potential to become a story. Your hobbies, pets, children, friends and enemies play a role in the inspiration of ideas. It begins with a single sentence or a visual image and grows to become the basis for the plot of your story.

Everything that has happened to you in your lifetime can be developed. Life is often a parable for art.

2. DAYDREAMS

Daydreams can become as much as part of your life as memories. Each of your fantasies can be turned into a story. Boys dream about becoming a cowboy, a fireman, a super hero. The action story is born. The trappings of historical novels may be borrowed from research but the author is still there, walking the streets, riding in carriages, and wearing fancy clothes.

More of a writer's personality goes into his work than he knows. Characters act out dreams and desires, and reflect the secret passions of the author. A writer whose stories are laced with a large amount of violence may be so mild mannered he wouldn't step on a bug, but it is doubtful whether these scenes could be created without him ever having a violent thought.

3. FACT

Writers compulsively save bits of information they find in newspapers, magazines, and books. The data is filed until it emerges as an action story, a crime drama, or a heart-tugging human interest piece.

Sometimes, several pieces of data can be woven together to form one story. You may have found an article about the courage of a farm woman, another about a flood, still another about a mother risking her life to save a child. Each of these news reports can be used to build one story about a farm woman whose child's life was threatened by a flash-flood. The ingredients for an excellent action drama, and the potential for many endings, are there.

4. LETTERS TO THE EDITOR/ADVICE COLUMNS

Many excellent ideas can be found in the letters people write, whether for advice or opinion. The Letters To the Editor section of the newspaper presents emotion, raw nerves and strong opinion. Advice columns are filled with human interest drama.

5. BOOK TITLES

Have you ever picked up a book only to find it is nothing like the title implies? You have stumbled upon an idea for a story: your initial perception. The title, BRIDESMAID, can suggest a story about an older woman who has lost all hope of marriage; a story about a young woman anticipating her own marriage; a mystery about a bridesmaid who is sure the bride is making a mistake and sets out to prove it. The limits exist only within your imagination.

6. TELEVISION

Many ideas turn up on television. I'm not talking about plagiarism, where you write down everything you see. That's breaking copyright and it's illegal. I'm talking about watching something that triggers a memory or sparks an idea for a similar plot with a completely different ending.

7. CONVERSATION

People tell you all sorts of things—especially when they find out you are a writer. There's a mystique around the profession that encourages people to share experiences. I can't count the number of times someone has said to me, "I have the best idea for you," or "You should write a story about this."

Conversations you overhear on a bus, in stores and banks, anywhere people collect, supply you with more ideas than you can use.

I'll never forget the day I was sitting across from an elderly lady riding alone on a bus. Her clothes were mended, her hat was outdated and her shoes needed repair, but she was clean and she was filled with dignity.

She sat quietly, clutching a worn cloth bag that held one loaf of day-old bread. She didn't see the two designer-dressed teens who slid into the seat behind her, but she did hear their taunts and their laughter. One tear, as lonely as the lady, carved a path down her cheek.

The lady inspired THE GIFT, a short story published in a family living magazine.

Conversations you have with other people provide insight into feelings, help you "hear" speech patterns, and give you ideas for plotlines.

8. EDITORS

Once a publication is regularly accepting your work it is not unusual for the editor to give you ideas. He knows your work and recognizes you as a professional so, when a special story is needed, you may just get a call.

9. BOOKS

Reading is probably the single best source for ideas. As your memory is stimulated, you relate to the characters and recall locations and background. There is the added benefit of learning from another writer's technique. Before you can be a successful writer, you must learn to be an avid reader.

As you read, make a note of what worked and what did not—and why. Write down characters' strengths and weaknesses. Outline the scenes that filled you with emotion.

If you didn't like the ending, jot down why and what you would have done instead. List the plot twists you might have added and analyze their importance in the story. Every book you read should add something to your craft.

10. HISTORY

History can be turned into fiction, whether it is your personal history or general world history. My maternal grandmother was a "purchased bride", arriving alone in North America at the age of thirteen to a life and man unknown to her. She has been an endless source for fiction.

Battles fought hundreds of years ago, mores of a time long past, plagues, natural disasters and unsolved mysteries are all grist for the mill. Looking for an idea? Open a history book.

Ideas have to be given time to develop. It's fine to see something and know there is a story in it, but it is important to let it rumble around in your head and heart until it matures. If you write a story too soon, the plot will be thin and the characters two dimensional.

Once you learn to recognize ideas, you'll find yourself drowning in the paper war. The time has come to develop a filing system. The following is only a suggestion, a place to start. Experiment and find what works best for you.

You have been clipping from newspapers and magazines everything that can be turned into fiction. You have carried a pad and noted conversations, locations, buildings, parks, people, events—anything that can be supporting material as well as the base for a plotline. Now you'll need a place to keep all these bits of information.

If you have the room, and the finances, for a good filing cabinet then that's the route to take. If you can't afford a metal cabinet, then good file-boxes are the next best thing. They can be stacked, are easily stored, and are sturdy enough to be moved around. I have both—a two-drawer metal cabinet and file boxes.

The cabinet holds the active files, including correspondence, submissions, and sales files. The boxes hold reference material, hard copies of all manuscripts, and inactive files.

If file-boxes are not available or affordable then heavy cardboard boxes, often given free at grocery stores, work fine. Buy or make folders that can be labelled and placed alphabetically in the box.

The easiest way for me to set up an "ideas file" is to do it by category. I have a folder for children's fiction, mystery, romance, history, and so on. If these files get out of hand, I divide them again. For example, history can be subdivided into periods; mystery into murder, robbery, fraud, etc.

A card file, with numbered cross-reference, helps you locate material quickly. For example, the card heading reads HISTORY. Listed and numbered on the card is each piece of reference material you have on hand. The clippings and notes in the file are numbered to correspond with the card.

The trick is to stay organized—keep the numbers in sequence as you file and refile.

Remember, when you are building your files, to include pictures. An old house, a spectacular outfit, a basket full of bunnies—everything that stirs an emotion in you will also stir your reader when you put the picture into words.

You may never use all the ideas you save but a good filing system, filled with interesting clippings, will prove to be one of your most valuable tools.

Keep in mind that not every idea is going to work for you. Some do not fall within your realm of experience. Some will not interest you. Others do not have enough depth to stand on their own.

From the one-liner comes the idea and from the idea comes the plot. The hard part is gathering all your thoughts and changing them, in a correlated and logical manner, into thousands of words.

CHAPTER TWO

OUTLINES

One of the most important tools for a beginning writer is the outline. It is the pattern by which all things are built. Outlines are guides. They give you confidence. They put you in touch with your characters and the directions you want them to take. Deviations occur when the people you've created don't want to do what they're told.

My reaction, the first time I heard a writer say the characters had minds of their own, or that the story didn't end the way he expected it to, was one of disbelief. I was convinced this was some kind of mystique fiction writers nurtured to proliferate the myth surrounding them. I changed my mind when the hero of my own story stamped his foot and said, I'm not going to do that. It's completely out of character!

So why bother with an outline? There are several reasons: It gives you a place to start, thereby helping to remove the blank page syndrome; there is no better way to get to know your characters; the action, conflicts and resolutions become clear in your mind.

Departures from the outline occur in character reaction, dialogue, motivation of secondary characters and plot twists. They do not usually occur in major plot developments if the outline has been thoroughly thought out.

A detailed outline becomes the seed from which your story germinates to carry its own principles of growth. It will draw from your subconscious, in a process of intelligent selection, vast amounts of experience. People will come together in places, with times and dates and weather and scenery. You will see a world for them, complete with stumbling blocks and champions.

A story seldom presents itself as a whole. The outline helps you see the whole before you write yourself into situations you cannot resolve. We've all been faced with an unsatisfactory conclusion or characters that disappear without explanation. We've all experienced the empty feelings and frustrations that often result from this kind of writing.

My way of dealing with an outline is simple and it works for me. Once an idea has presented itself and simmered until there is something to work with, I begin by jotting down names of characters and bits of action. Next, I do a study of each character. Included are physical features, age, emotional traits (weaknesses and strengths), relationships, dreams and desires. A bio is completed for everyone appearing in the story, no matter how minor.

This is a valuable device in the construction of fiction. Your characters do come alive and they will take off on their own as they move through your story. It is this detailed knowledge and understanding that enables you to give your characters life.

When you start your outline, it will amaze you how little you know about your plot but, as you work, it begins to reveal itself. Action expands in excitement, characters take on personality, and areas that were vague become clear. By the time you write your first draft, most of the puzzles are solved.

The length of the outlines will vary with subject and format. Too complicated an outline will defeat your purpose; too brief and you may as well not bother. The following suggestion is a place to start. Modify it and make it your own.

1. The purpose of the story. Never lose sight of what it is you set out to do. What emotion do you want to stimulate in your reader? What is the theme of your story? Remember, the theme is the point you wish to make. It poses a question or sets out a problem.

The theme may be as simple as "crime never pays" or as complex as the theory of war. It is a natural, unobtrusive part of the story; the quality that carries a sense of values and brings drama to the writing.

2. What is the key character's motivation? In a romance, the motivation is love. In a mystery, it can be greed, passion, revenge, jealousy—any of the human emotions that overrides human lives. Before you begin to plot your action, you must know what it is that motivates your character. He must have a purpose that makes the action run parallel to the incentive.

3. What obstacles will the key character face? List the conflicts and problems in the order you expect them to happen. For each, introduce the initial clash, build that clash to a mini-climax, and state the key character's reaction to the event.

Good fiction, unless it is a short-short, will have more than one conflict. Listing them in order of occurrence ensures that struggles will increase in intensity as the story progresses. The final conflict, and its outcome, is the resolution of the plot.

The conflicts, as they appear, should give you the basis for your plot. Plot is simply the series of events that proves or disproves the point (theme) of the story.

4. Resolution. Each conflict will carry its own resolution but it is the final one that is the conclusion of the story. The final conflict must come logically from those that preceded it, therefore making the final resolution satisfying to the reader.

If you quickly resolve your plot twists without fully explaining what happened and why, your reader will never forgive you.

Once you have the outline for your characters and their conflicts, the next step is to develop the background. Often, too little emphasis is placed on this important element in the writing process.

Background is more than the scenery we pull by. It is the environment in which the characters live their lives. It is their past and their future. They are what they are because of it. Events happen because of background. Characters act in a certain way because they live in a certain place under certain conditions. If you can place your people in another location and have them act and react in the same way, then you are not using your background effectively.

One trick is setting the scene for the character and not for the reader. Another is to forget what you want—what does the character want? It is imperative that you know your characters and the events that shaped every facet of their being.

Above all, remember that your outline is a guide. It can, and probably will, be changed.

CHAPTER THREE

BUILDING CHARACTERS

The outline is done, the main scenes are planned, and the plot is clear in your mind so you start to write. Then you read the first few pages and everything seems to have died. The story is nothing but a string of words and you have no idea what's wrong. You started before you got to know your characters.

You must know each one well enough to make them part of your life before you begin your first draft. If you try to get to know them as you work, you will be faced with an endless string of revisions, removing the inconsistencies and contradictions in logic. Save yourself an immeasurable amount of time and energy. Do a bio for each person in your story.

This is not the dreary task it may seem. It is a journey through life and the things you discover will surprise you. These revelations set the tone of the relationships, define the personalities and present the motivation for your action.

To make the story move, the characters must grow and change. At first, they are presented to the reader with all their flaws and self-delusions. They hide their true feelings. They rationalize and manipulate. In every scene, somebody does something, wants something or gets something. While this is happening, the reader also gets something—information.

The majority of new writers find the process of getting to know their people, difficult. They try to pattern them after someone they know and occasionally it works, but more often it does not. They try not to let too much of themselves come through. The work they produce is stilted.

They build imaginary people and make sure the editor knows exactly how each one looks, and that he closed the door when he left the room. They say that the clothing was blue and the house white with green trim. Everything external is covered.

The story is mailed, along with the conviction there will be a sale. Then, the submission comes back with a comment along the lines of, Round out your characters! It's hair-tearing time. They would be delighted to round out everything if they only knew how.

I do a written interview with every character, no matter how small the part. I ask him questions about his childhood and family relationships; about friends, past and present. I find out what he likes and dislikes and what his dreams are for the future.

I question him about those things in himself he admires—and loathes. I want to know if he likes his job, the people he works with, chocolate milk. I ask him outrageous questions knowing many answers will never be used. But they help me know my character.

Conduct this interview the same way you would with a real person. Answer the questions in first person. Wear two hats! The interviewer asks: What do you like about yourself? The character answers: I am loyal and honest—at least, I try to be honest . . . and so on. Let yourself go and let the character really answer the questions as he sees them. The outcome will amaze you.

There are three requirements your protagonist must fill. He needs to be sympathetic, original, and credible.

When a major character is unsympathetic, the reader loses interest, mainly because he cannot get caught up in his fate. Being sympathetic does not mean saintly. In fact, the opposite is likely true. The character flaws are the ingredients that add humanity to your people.

When the character is lacking in originality, the reader's ability to identify is strained. If he has met the same type of person repeatedly, there is no freshness left. There is nothing to bring the character to life. Why should the reader care what happens to him?

A mistake frequently made by a novice is confusing character tags with characterization. He tells his reader that the character's name is Winnie, that she's 68 years old, that she hennas her hair. Winnie likes to sleep late and have breakfast in bed. She likes her cat and is shy with people.

What we have here is a series of labels, not a picture of the person. You need more than a sum of the physical attributes to make an enduring character. You need a personality. How she acts and reacts, how she sees the world and survives in it, is more important than the fact that she colours her hair.

The major character must be furnished with idiosyncrasies that make him stand out from all the rest of the people in this story, and any other your audience has read. You need to give him a history that has shaped his life.

Your character needs to do things that no one else does. Maybe our Winnie likes to hang out at a lunch counter, spending no money but sipping water, because she loses the feeling of loneliness without having to talk to anyone. You need to tell the reader why the owner lets her do this, and why people frighten her.

When you know your characters so well that you confuse them with the real people in your life, you won't have any trouble making them believable. They

will walk through your pages as naturally as you walk through your day.

Good characters will "take off on their own" and do unexpected things. Some will delight you. Others will annoy you because they changed your story, forcing you to revise the outline.

They live in a specific time, reacting to what has happened and what is about to happen. You must know each character's dilemma and how he will resolve it emotionally. Believable characters have mystery and power.

Choose one gesture and emphasize it. Give him a dominant feature. Keep your character consistent and never force anything on him. If you do, you'll end up with a stereotype. Listen when he speaks to you!

A character that's too good to be true is seldom believable. He needs flaws, physical and moral, to be realistic. I'm not referring to the Seven Deadly Sins, but those everyday things in a person's life that he is not willing to admit to.

There are the flaws we try to hide from ourselves, or lack the wisdom to see. There are the personality traits that we accept and ignore because it's more comfortable that way. Then there are the flaws we try to correct, the ones that translate into growth.

The best characterization emerges, from an in depth bio, as the story is being written. It surpasses every trait you assign because it comes from knowing who your people are. However, it is possible to be so close to a character that you remove all the flaws. You identify with the good and hide the bad.

The writer needs to distance himself from the character. One way to do this is to select a stranger, someone you see at the bus stop or in the food store or at the bowling alley, to use as a pattern. Another trick is to recruit a minor character in the story, one who dislikes your flawless hero, to present a second version.

A character without flaws has nowhere to go. He can't change or grow. He cannot involve himself with the lives of others because he has no empathy. He is not real.

Minor characters must be as carefully cast as the protagonists. Bios must be done. You need to know how they walk and talk and think—even if they never say a word.

Avoid the photographic image: He was six feet, two inches, with dark hair and eyes. His mouth was full and, when he smiled, his teeth showed even and white.

There is nothing of the person in this description. The character needs to be doing something to let the reader "see" his physical and emotional traits. Let's have another look at the same paragraph.

He stood, filling the doorway with his six foot, two inch frame. Wind-whipped, black hair fell in strands that threatened his prominent brows. Dark eyes telegraphed his anger as he scanned the room in search of the woman who had eluded him. Suddenly, the anger lifted and his full lips parted in a radiant smile. He sighed. He had found her.

Now the character is more than hair colouring and height. He has been somewhere. You know his emotional state. You know his quest. And you are close to knowing the resolution. You still know his hair colour and his height!

Characters need names. Sometimes they come to you easily but most of the time they do not. While the success of the story doesn't depend on the names you give your people, those names can influence how the editor and the reader feel about what you have written.

The choice is yours, but be aware of the pitfalls.

1. Don't use names of real people. Sometimes, a name will pop into your head. It has a marvellous ring to it and fits your character perfectly. If a name sounds too good, check an encyclopedia and a copy of Who's Who. You may have selected something that seemed right because it is familiar.

2. Choose interesting names. Names that are common in real life are colourless in fiction. Bob Smith, action hero, isn't

going to inspire a reader. Names do reflect personalities and stimulate images, so choose carefully.

Books of names, intended for new parents, are a help. Television guides, magazines and novels, are sources. Be inventive in combining the first and last names to avoid real people or well-known fictional characters.

First names can be interesting. Imaginative, uncomplicated spellings (Caryn/Karen) and surnames used as first names (Sterling, Wilson, Walker), add drama. The use of a hyphenated name such as Henderson Wilson-Smythe, endows the character with status and wealth.

Keep a notebook and stockpile interesting names for future use.

3. Avoid confusion. There are few things more annoying than reading a story containing names that all begin with the same letter—like Carol, Carl, and Carrie. True, it happens in real life but in fiction it doesn't make sense. The same applies to names that rhyme. Calling your hero, Andy and your heroine, Sandie, and the minor characters Hal and Al, is going to make it difficult for your readers to keep everyone straight.

4. Make the names easy to read. The search for interesting names does not mean creating ones that are impossible to pronounce. A reader does not want to stop and try to figure out how you say it. Putting your reader in the position of having to skip the name every time he comes to it, breaks the stride and threatens the reality.

5. Avoid "cute". Inventing interesting names is one thing. Going overboard, is another. We all grew up with Virginia Hamm, April Showers, and Ina Bird. Ice Blu may be a great name for an exotic dancer but it can't be used for the girl next door.

Names do add to the character's personality. They can show strength or weakness. Homer is likely the bespectacled boy, sitting at the front of the class. He is not believable as the Captain of the football team.

"Cute" names should only be used when your fiction is not to be taken seriously. Who can ever forget Ian Flemming's Pussy Galore?

WRITING THE BIO

1. Name and age

2. Height and weight, physical traits

3. Hair, eye, and skin colouring

4. Occupation

5. Family members

6. Friends

7. Background

Suggested Interview Questions

1. Tell me about your background. Where you were born, where you went to school, your family and friends.

2. What do you like about yourself?

3. What don't you like about yourself?

4. What are you keeping a secret?

5. How well do you know yourself?

6. Do you deceive yourself about anything?

7. A friend described your personality. How was he wrong? Right?

8. In what situation is your self-esteem at risk?

9. What frightens you?

10. When are you brave?

11. How well do your friends know you?

12. How has your life affected your personality?

13. What do you want from life?

14. What do you need to overcome?

15. What in the outside world is preventing you?

16. What in yourself is preventing you?

17. What must happen for you to overcome this?

18. How are you different with family than friends? 19. Who are you attracted to? Why?

20. What do you think he/she could do for you that no one else can?

21. What is your initial reaction to a stranger?

22. Do you try to charm or deceive people you meet?

23. How are you with rivals?

24. Who are your rivals?

25. What do you first notice when you walk into a room?

26. How do you see the world?

27. How do you learn best?

28. How do you decide if you can trust someone?

29. What are your goals in life?

30. Describe yourself to me.

Take time to construct solid characters. They are going to be responsible for everything that happens in your story. You cannot even begin to think about writing until every one of your people is so real that you speak of them as you would any member of the family.

CHAPTER FOUR

DIALOGUE

There is no more important component of fiction than dialogue. Good characters and natural dialogue, that speaks to the ear as well as the mind, advances and defines the plot and makes complicated developments, believable.

Many beginning writers do not place enough emphasis on dialogue. They believe the strength of the story is in the narrative, forgetting that if the characters do not have a strong voice they have no quality, temperament, or identity.

There are two basic methods: short dialogue and exposition dialogue. Short dialogue is made up of single, concise sentences. It is written much the same way as people talk. For example:

"Where are you going?"

"To the store?"

"Which One?"

"The market on Fifth."

"Will you bring me some peanuts?"

"Sure. If you're paying."

Expository dialogue gives each speaker more than a line or two and may take on the characteristics of narrative. Unless a writer is accomplished, it can be difficult to write.

The sequence has to be charted in advance rather than allowing the exchange to flow naturally. Most people do not speak in intricate sentences and paragraphs. They lose interest in what they are saying, or run out of ideas, and wait for someone else to reply.

Expository dialogue is useful when unravelling a complicated plot. The famous detective gathers everyone in the parlour, stands before a roaring fire, and expounds for pages as he reveals who did the dastardly deed.

Good dialogue does not need speaker identification for every line. We all use overworked phrases, double negatives, and punctuate sentences with favourite cliches. Speech traits, written properly, show the reader who is talking.

I'm not saying that every character's dialogue should be loaded with idiomatic features. The key is using them sparingly to make the conversation seem less contrived.

Fictional characters should not rely on bad English and phonetically spelled words to show lack of education or intelligence. While they should be made to speak realistically, dropping g's, and the excessive use of gonna, c'mon, yer, ya, and so on, can become tiresome to the reader.

The same applies to the use of dialect. Suggested, rather than phonetically written dialogue, does not stop the flow of the story. Sparsely used, it shows the character's ethnic background. Overuse it and you irritate the reader.

Don't use slang or jargon that will soon be dated or expressions that apply only to a small part of the world. Also, make sure the style you are using suits the character uttering the words. You don't want a cultured, seventy-year-old matriarch saying, Button yer lip.

Tag words are the "said" substitutes. There is nothing wrong with said but new writers seem to spend too much time trying to get rid of it. Often their dialogue is loaded with hissed, sneered, gulped, spat, rasped, gurgled, croaked, bubbled and fumed.

Indiscriminate use of tag words weakens good dialogue. Even such words as asked, answered, replied, questioned, whispered and shouted, should not be constantly repeated.

Another often-made-mistake, is using verbs for tag words. "That's a funny hat," Bob laughed. Bob did not laugh the words . . . he said the words and then he laughed. The sentence should have read, "That's a funny hat," Bob said, with a laugh.

Adverbs are used when a character does more than say something. Slowly, warily, carefully, happily, sadly, are some familiar words. When used in moderation they're fine, but remember, no one uses an inflection or expresses an emotion every time he speaks.

Tag words are the accents in dialogue. Like all emphasis, the less frequently they are used, the more effective they become. Tag words also serve a purpose when a meaning needs clarifying. A whisper is different from a shout.

"Come over here," John whispered are words spoken with love. "Come over here," John shouted are words spoken in anger. Had the author simply written: "Come over here," the interpretation would not be clear.

Perhaps the easiest way to learn dialogue is to practise "talking" to the paper. Write imaginary scenes and exchanges. Work out your own problems by giving them to characters for discussion. Use every mood and every emotion, and keep doing it until it is effortless.

Once you can write conversations as if they are happening, it is time to consider the voice that tells the story . . . the Point of View.

POV is a central feature of a story's composition and the only element present from beginning to end. A commanding voice will compensate for many weaknesses in dialogue, setting, narrative and characterization. However, if the voice that speaks to the reader is inadequate, it won't matter how well-rounded your characters, or how exotic your settings, the story will not be strong.

There are two basic voices in fiction: first- and third-person persona. Mastering the technique can result in infinite variations of effect. Before you select the voice, ask yourself:

a) Who will be the narrator? The author, in first- or third-person? A character, in first- or third-person? An omniscient narrator?

b) From what angle does the narrator tell the story? Front, centre, above, periphery, or shifting?

c) Where are you going to place the reader? In the story, away from the story, or shifting?

Sometimes, the writer instinctively adopts a viewpoint position and the story goes well. Other times, he finds he is bogged down in explanations, or that he is reaching resolutions too soon, or the best scenes are happening "offstage".

The problems likely stem from the choice of viewpoint. The author's attitude toward the character can help determine the angle from which he views him.

FIRST-PERSON POINT OF VIEW

The use of the I voice is the most comfortable one for new writers because it is an imaginative extension of the voice they use in writing letters and essays. It is known as First-person Narrative.

If the story is told in the first-person through a character, then it is the character's voice that is always present. The writer must know the character's every thought, act and feeling; his conscious and unconscious life; his wants, needs and motivations.

In fiction, the voice is tailored to fit the requirements of characterization. The voice "creates" a character that must be consistent throughout the story. It can only tell what the character already knows. The persona reflects gender, age, social status, education, heritage and emotional makeup.

In this voice, the fictional account of an event is told as if it really happened. Frequently, the story has a base in personal experience. The writer has the privilege of adding, combining, or eliminating characters, altering their traits, and changing the background.

Exaggeration builds drama and suspense. The writer shapes the conclusion into what he thinks should have happened. First person stories are used in every genre—romance, mystery, general or literary—but the style varies with each.

THIRD-PERSON

A third-person persona has no personal identity so the writer does not have to concern himself with gender, age, education, etc. This persona is not a "character" in the sense that first-person is but, it exhibits character. There is an emotional and intellectual level of comment and thought.

The author centres everything around the life of the main character. He follows only what that character sees, hears, feels and thinks. The reader begins to identify with the character and to care about what happens to him.

In this voice, the dialogue is in first-person but narration, told by the author, is in third-person.

There are at least five first-person and six third-person voices, some rarely used. Concern yourself with the common usage, and learn the subtleties by doing.

Viewpoint in not as simple as choosing a character, or a position, and then telling the story through his mind and feelings. Viewpoint is alive. The author puts himself inside the character and lives with him. He must become the viewpoint character; living the way he lives, doing the things the character would do, and he must never contradict the character traits.

Before the writer takes a viewpoint position, he would be wise to examine his own personality. What are his limitations? His strengths and weaknesses? Taking into consideration which character he identifies with, will help determine how the story will best be told.

No choice is more important than point of view. Trial and error may be necessary before the writer makes the final decision as to persona. Stories become believable because the voices that tell the stories compel belief.

A reader is unlikely to believe an uncommitted, flat third-person voice. Nor will he be persuaded by an inconsistent first-person persona.

You will hear, Write what you know, physically and emotionally, many times over. It is some of the best advice a new writer can be given because work connected to personal experience is unique. No one else has your background.

You will find your own voice. Use it with authority. It is your vision of life.

CHAPTER FIVE

STYLE

Mystery and misunderstanding surround the word style. It comes from the tendency to stress the importance of individual style instead of looking at the definition in a broader sense. The word becomes a puzzle when a writer thinks of it of as his style, forgetting it is the style of the story, as well.

This imbalance leads beginning writers to believe they must work to develop a method that will set their writing apart from all others. Individual style is the manner of expression peculiar to a specific writer. It develops from his own personality, from his attitudes and motivations, and from his background. Style is the writer.

However, it does not happen automatically. New writers need to think about style and to be conscious of other writer's techniques. Reading short fiction is one of the best sources of guidance, providing you are aware of the tendency to imitate.

Experienced writers seldom read the same genre while they are writing. Plot development, dialogue, characterization, narrative and descriptions, can carry over into their work without them even knowing it.

Read, analyze, and be aware of a strong style, but don't try to copy it—no matter how much you admire the author. Understand why it works and use the information to find the trouble spots in your own writing.

It is necessary to bring together form and substance. They must be inseparable. The words we use, and the way we use them, determine the strengths and weakness of the story.

Form, the adaptation of the expression to the idea, conveys the substance. It is the means by which something is made identifiable. An undeveloped thought is not communicated. An inadequately defined character does not live. A poorly expressed emotion does not touch the reader.

Words are the molecular structure of the written piece. We all use the same words, but the way they are put together and arranged is what constitutes our style and the art of our writing.

The first step in development, is to fully understand the rules of grammar. Art is not fixed and absolute; the rules of grammar are. Unless you grasp the basics behind the structure, you will not cultivate the instincts that say, this word is better than that one.

Sentence structure is an important part of style.

Sentences are made up of single, complete thoughts. They can be as short as one word or as long as a paragraph. There are no arbitrary rules that govern sentence length, but simplicity is favoured over complexity. It is safest to stay moderate, saving very short or very long sentences for some special purpose.

Short sentences give a dramatic effect, speed up action and are useful for emphasis. However, if the effect you want is not achieved, a series of short sentences will sound undeveloped and immature.

The long sentence also has special uses. If the thought is complex, there should be no break in continuity. Long sentences build mood, seek the revelations of a character's mind, and emphasise descriptive passages.

But, here too, there are dangers. If the sentence is so interwoven with thought that it loses the reader along the way, you run the risk of losing him forever. Too many long sentences in a row make it difficult for your reader to follow the plot. The writing can become bombastic.

Incomplete sentences are fractional in themselves but they express a complete thought. Any part of a sentence—a phrase, a subordinate clause, a single word—can stand as a sentence. Used sparingly, they are effective dramatic tools.

Sentences are strung together into paragraphs. A paragraph is more than a break on the page. It is a unit made up of several related sentences that moves the reader forward. Only those details that support one principal theme should be included.

The sentences that make up the paragraph are carefully arranged, varying in length, form, and sound. They should not begin with the same word unless the writer is using repetition for emphasis.

Repetition requires careful construction. It can be very effective if the writer has the ability to make the reader understand what he is doing. If not, repetition tends to be dull.

Computer grammar-check programmes go a long way in simplifying a writer's life. Not only do they point out errors in spelling and structure, they collect statistics and exhibit errors in style.

People read fiction for entertainment. They escape into the lives of characters from exotic cultures and from different times. They read fiction to feel, in the context of safety.

The writer's style is the yardstick of the reader's experience. To make him part of the bank robbery, the capturing of a pirate ship, or the love interest of the protagonist, the writer's style must be strong enough to bring the characters to life and, therefore, rouse powerful feelings in the reader.

Your self-knowledge is the primary source for everything you create. If you are going to write a story about a crime, you must find that place within yourself where, under given circumstances, you are capable of committing that crime.

Often, the feelings that set off the strongest stories are the ones you do not yet understand. An idea comes to you, excites you, and you know this is the theme and plot you want to do. You feel it is right but do not understand your reasons for responding in such a positive way.

It doesn't matter why you care. It matters that you do care—and strongly. Lack of emotion will leave the story flat and your reader uninvolved. If you do not cry over the sadness in the story, or laugh at the humour, neither will your audience.

Translating this emotion into good writing depends on good style. You may be feeling a great deal for your character and his plight, but if you lack the technical strength to express that to the reader, it will not garner a response.

Good fiction is not a catharsis. It is not a vehicle for exposing the soul. Nor is it a method of inflicting your views, to the point of preaching, on your reader. The core comes from some level within yourself, a place where you are still struggling, but it is assembled from the most accessible regions of your imagination.

Don't be alarmed if your first attempts at fiction are intensely autobiographical. These stories will likely remain unpublished because there is a self-indulgence that fails to evoke a reader response. What they do, however, is help to develop style. The more you write, the more you can distance yourself from the events and the people. It is then that you begin to write fiction that carries its own style.

If you want your readers to feel, start with what you feel most strongly about. Mould those feelings until you have shaped them into something that will make your reader laugh or cry or sigh with relief.

Adopt, either the preference to tell the story boldly and directly, or to act upon the reader's feelings. Take the middle ground and your work will lack strength.

There is no satisfactory explanation of style or guide to good writing. Every writer displays an individual style that involves his method of presentation and his expression of ideas. It may be good or bad.

Style is developed through practise and the mastery of grammatical techniques. Effectiveness can be determined by: the writer's inherent use of viewpoint, acceptability from the reader's viewpoint, and the suitability of the content.

Style is best described as your specific way of using language.

CHAPTER SIX

TITLES

Every story needs a working title. It is unlikely it will be used when the manuscript finds its way to print, but there is something about the act of typing words at the top of the page that gives you a starting point.

A strong story can find an audience, with or without a good title. Similarly, the most intriguing title in the world won't sell a badly written piece. But a title is the first thing an editor sees, so it pays to give it your attention.

Initially, my interest is putting something down that will identify the story. Somewhere, between the beginning and the end of the manuscript, a phrase, a word, or a sentence will likely pop up and be the perfect title.

If this doesn't happen, then I brainstorm when the story is completed. The title for The Purchased Bride, began with, Necessity For Life, my working title. The story of a Hungarian immigrant alone, and lonely, farming in Southern Alberta in the early 1900s, is a tender one.

Recalling a little girl from his home village years before, my Hungarian wrote to her family and finally arranged a purchase. She arrived in Canada, frightened and unable to remember the man her family said she knew. Trials were many, but they were overcome and the story ended happily.

On completion, I didn't like the title and began the brainstorming process. I first read the manuscript, searching for a word or phrase that would say what I wanted it to, but there was nothing.

Next, I began to write a list of titles as they came to mind. A Necessary Part of Life, A Man's Desire, The Farm Wife, The Bride, and finally, The Purchased Bride.

The title you give your story is probably the least important factor in determining a sale. An editor knows it can be changed. Still, it is wise to try to come up with something sensational. As I said before, it is the first thing the editor—and the reader—sees. A title should whet the appetite.

1. Make the title memorable. You want to avoid trite "label" titles like The House, The Cat, My Horse, Jennifer, The Challenge, and so on. Short titles work better than long ones because they are more easily remembered.

2. Make the title fit the story. A good title illustrates the theme of the story. It tells you if it is a mystery, a western, a romance, etc. It hints at the plot without revealing too much of it. The Ten-year-old Boy Who Took His Dog For A Walk In The Woods, is just about the worst title I can think of.

3. Avoid unpronounceable words and unknown data. The story may have an ethnic flavour or contain material unfamiliar to the average reader. In context, the obscure are made clear but, as a title, all remains a mystery. Play it safe and choose something everyone can understand.

4. Be careful with puns. Puns can be clever but they can also be annoying. If you insist on using a pun as a title, be sure it clearly tells what the story is about and that it is not trite.

A writer gets a feel for titles the longer he works. Words jump out at you and sentences and phrases present themselves as you read your manuscript. Keeping a notebook of disembodied titles can be a help. You never know where or when they will be useful.

Remember—titles can, and likely will, be changed.

SECTION TWO

CHAPTER SEVEN

THE SHORT STORY

Fiction falls into several categories. A writer takes personal experience, history, true crime, and turns them into stories to delight a reader. From the imagination comes romance, mystery, science fiction, and the fantasy created for children.

All short fiction is loosely labelled short story, but there is a marked difference in length, format and market selection according to the genre. This section is going to look at the classifications, define the structure and guide you in placing the finished work.

Before we can get into the specifics, you need to understand the concept of short fiction. It is from here that all forms grow.

WRITING THE SHORT STORY

The short story is an account of a distinct piece of action. The plot can be inspired by fact, come entirely from the writer's imagination, or be a combination of fact and fiction.

Short stories can be traced back to King Cheops, the great Egyptian pyramid builder. It is said the king would gather his sons around the throne and tell them tales of magicians from times long past.

One of the earliest known collections of short stories is, Tales of the Magicians, also originating in Egypt approximately five thousand years ago. In the Middle Ages, the short story took the form of the beast fables, and contained morals.

Edgar Allen Poe was the first to establish rules for short fiction. He stipulated that a story must reach for only one effect and have the values of time, mood, space and action.

Historically, the short story was the weapon of priests and magicians, and the art of reformers since before the time of Buddha. Even today, there are primitive tribes whose mysteries, legends and customs are passed down only in short story form.

What exactly is a short story? How long should a story be? My answer to that question has always been long enough to tell it. True, markets have their individual preferences dictated by space. It then becomes your job to tailor your work to their editorial needs.

Market sources and guidelines divide submission information into vignette, short-short, short, and novella lengths. As a rule, the vignette is any piece with less than 1000 words. Short-shorts are between 1000 and 2000 words. Short stories are 2,000-7500 words but can be up to 15,000 words, and novellas (mini-novels) are a maximum of 40,000 words.

A vignette is a short piece of writing intended to convey an image of a character, scene, or situation. Fiction, in this form, is often based on fact or personal profile. Properties of the vignette are precise phrase construction and an emotional tone.

The short-short is the best way to tell a story consisting of an uncomplicated, single incident with an unpredictable ending. It must be entered into directly, require no build-up, have minimal background, and characters with only enough biography to move the story quickly to the end.

A short story generally revolves around a situation or a character with a problem to solve. The method the author uses, to help him solve the problem, is the plot. The point the author wants to make is the theme. There must be enough character development for the protagonist to change, for better or for worse.

The short story format allows you more latitude in the construction of plot and theme, and contains as many characters and scenes as is necessary to the plot. However, the time span is still limited so there is no room for superfluous characters and scenes.

The Novella, an Italian term meaning story, is a relatively short piece of fiction, running in length from 7,000-40,000 words. Typically, it is published as a separate unit by small press publishers. The Old Man and the Sea is an example of this genre.

There is magic in telling a good story through the written word. Weaving that magic is the responsibility of the author. He must grab the reader's attention, take him by the hand and lead him through a world that exists only in his imagination. This is the technique you are striving to master. When you do, you become part of the magic.

But how do you keep your readers riveted to the page? The writer, deprived of the audience communication he enjoyed when stories were told orally, often finds himself detached from his readers. He must work to keep in constant touch and one way of doing this is to remember the following guidelines.

1. Assess the story before you start. How do you feel about the plot and theme? Does it grab you? If your answer is no, forget it. If you aren't captivated by the storyline, the people, and the action, you cannot expect to hold your reader. Write only those stories you feel compelled to write and write from the heart.

2. Don't write to be "commercial." You heard "sex sells" so you sit down to write a steamy story. You find you are terribly uncomfortable with the format but you press on. After all, it will pay big bucks, won't it? No, it won't. If it sees print

at all, chances are it will reveal a contempt for the reader because you have not written for him—you have written for money.

3. Involve your reader. Start with a bang! Make your reader begin asking questions by the end of the first paragraph. Keep him turning pages by constructing a story that forces him to continue asking questions. Don't ramble. Sustain the suspense. Each scene must be absolutely necessary to the story; each character fully developed.

4. Use cliff-hangers. A cliff-hanger snaps the story to a halt, a technique used to jolt the reader and send him rushing toward the end because he can't wait to find out what will happen. The story needs to flow evenly before and after the cliff-hanger and transitions between scenes must be smooth. These "jolts of action" will lose their effectiveness if they are overused.

5. Create real people. It doesn't matter if you are writing a short-short with only one character, or a novella with several, the same rule applies. Your characters must be multi-dimensional people whom the reader will either love or love to hate. At the very least, the readers must feel involved and interested in the characters.

To accomplish this, you must love your characters but you must also be objective, seeing them with intelligent, unsentimental clarity. One of the worst mistakes a writer can make is to become so infatuated with his people he loses sight of their shortcomings. When that happens, they emerge as a mere caricature of weakness and strength.

People are a mixture of principles. The secret to presenting a real character is to balance good and bad traits within his personality.

6. Create logical conflicts. You have developed an exciting plot, put forth an interesting theme, and assembled a cast of multi-dimensional characters. Now you must give

these characters a difficult time and let your reader watch them work their way through it.

Often rejection letters contain the comment: the conflicts are contrived. Few things are more frustrating to a new writer than to have an editor make that statement.

You wrote in a problem. And the problem had a solution. Getting to that solution was tough for the protagonist. So what's the issue? Usually, the trouble starts with contradictions in logic.

A contradiction happens when a character does something that is out of context or against his personality. You would not write that an eighty-five year old man, using a walker, ran for the bus.

Contradictions in logic also occur when a writer switches hair or eye colour, forgets height or weight, or suddenly changes his character's dress in the middle of a scene. Careful character development, before you start, should eliminate these glaring errors.

Conflicts must be resolved in ways that are consistent with the protagonist's personality and in ways that are plausible to the reader. If they are not, the plot is not logical. It is contrived.

Contrived plots also occur when the motivation is not believable or is against the nature of the protagonist. Motivation must be logical. It must be intense enough to cause the conflict but it must not be so intense as to become absurd.

Sometimes, a new writer will throw in action for the sake of the action itself. It is not connected to anything that went before and has no connection to what will come after. But, hey—let's have a car chase! The story's a bit slow.

This kind of action never works and will likely elicit negative comments from the editor when the story is rejected. Action must move the plot. If it does not, it is contrived. It must affect the characters. If it does not, it is contrived. It must be real.

7.Many writers do not tell the story before it is written. Creativity is a pressure to tell a story and they find, once it is told, the urgency is gone; the artistic fever, cooled. You had a yarn to spin and you did that. You are creatively satisfied. When you do write the story, the quality and impact may be less than if you discovered it as you went along.

Fiction is made up of a beginning (setting up the conflict), a middle (the conflict itself) and an end (the resolution of the conflict).

THE BEGINNING

Every writer looks at the blank piece of paper or computer screen and moans, "Where do I start?" There are as many answers to that question as there are writers.

Some start with the first sentence and methodically work their way from beginning to end. Nothing will persuade them to leave their chosen path. Others start in the middle and write an action scene that puts them in touch with the characters and the theme. Some work around a particular piece of dialogue that came in a moment of inspiration. Still others write the final scenes, working backwards through the conflict.

As you gain experience, you'll find the best way for you. There are no rules but there are constants. The beginning of your story must have a strong hook that sets up the conflict and grabs your reader with a force that will not let go. Often you will find the plot dictates the way the opening paragraphs will be handled. If you are writing action/suspense, you will likely start with a fast-paced action scene. If you are writing romantic fiction, you will begin on an entirely different note.

Studying other authors' beginnings is a valuable exercise for a new writer. Make notes about what caught your attention and made you want to read on. When were the protagonists introduced? How was the action/conflict introduced? What worked and what did not?

The beginning must have shape—the pattern through which the story reveals itself. Is it comedic or tragic? Did it happen a long time ago or is it so immediate that the narrator is thinking aloud? Where did it happen? Is the story long or short? Description or dialogue driven?

Fictional shapes mirror the age in which they are written and are dictated to by the political and technological aspects of the decade. They are the footings that form the foundation of everything you write. Until you can move comfortably within the shape, you will not seriously get into the story.

A good first impression is essential, more so for the novice than for the established writer. When a story is submitted to an editor who is familiar with the author's work, he knows the story will probably improve if the beginning is not as strong as it could be. The editor also knows the author can rewrite to specification.

When an unknown writer submits a story with a weak beginning, it is unlikely that the editor will finish the manuscript. You'd better connect in the first paragraph or the risk of rejection is high. Without delay, get the story moving and set the tone by using action and image.

THE MIDDLE

This is the part of your story that carries the conflict and follows the protagonist as he tries to resolve the dilemma. Here is the heart of your story, the place where you involve the emotions, not the intellect, of your reader.

The "messages" are couched in drama. There is little rhetoric about the hero's state of mind; it is made clear by his actions. You are reaching your audience through behaviour and passion . . . not through the events in the story. When the protagonist's problem becomes the reader's problem, you will have accomplished what you set out to do. Your characters will live.

Initially, you create a situation—remorse, jealousy, disaster—and from the situation comes the plot. The longer the work, the more situations you have, so subplots begin to develop. Care must be taken not to lose sight of the predicament that determined the main action in the story.

The middle is based on a gradual upward swing moving towards the moment of recognition (the climax). Tension, created for its own sake, is weak. It needs to grow naturally from technique and be a means to an end—never the end itself.

Every story has its own pace. Some move slowly while others race towards the end. Transitions are the thrusts responsible for much of the movement. They connect one action to another. When successful, the reader is unaware of their presence.

There are three common transitions used in short stories: time, echo, and leapfrog.

TIME TRANSITION

Time transitions are the most common and the easiest to use. They are also the most obvious and can become dull. The purpose is to keep the reader chronologically oriented, moving in intervals of time that he can relate to and understand.

This transition becomes an art when it is used in a story where passing time is important. In this type of story, time passes in two levels. First, there is daily time—ages of children, the length of time it takes for a trip to a destination, etc. Second, there are flash-backs and flash-forwards.

We've lived here for five years now. The tree was planted a few weeks after we moved in. Next summer, it will give us its first fruit.

The paragraph shows time now . . . lived here five years now, flashes backward . . . was planted after we moved in, and forward . . . will give us its first fruit.

ECHO TRANSITION

Echo transitions are more interesting than time transitions. They link one part of the story to the next by repeating a word, activity or thought. They are swift and extremely useful in short story writing.

...starting part-time work. "The job doesn't pay much but it will give me a chance to meet someone." By the end of the week, Jennifer had met all kinds of men but they were either married, living with someone or completely incompatible. It wasn't until the end of the second month that she met the man she would marry.

The echo word is meet. In three sentences it takes you to Jennifer's job, through a series of introductions to unsuitable men, and finally to the man she will eventually marry.

LEAPFROG TRANSITION

Leapfrog transitions set up a scene, skip over it, and land in the next scene. It is the most difficult transition to write but it is interesting and forces the reader to participate in the action.

This transition is used in romantic fiction, for example, when the writer wants to skip over the seduction scene. The reader knows exactly what happened without the need to document the action.

Don't leapfrog any scene that is vital to the theme or plot. If a scene is essential, it must be written.

Conflict and action rely on the development of the characters. You did a profile, before you started to write, that put you in touch with the physical and emotional being. Now, ask yourself the following questions in relationship to the action and conflict.

1. What does the character fear?
2. What is the worst thing that can happen to him?
3. What one occurrence would throw his life into chaos?
4. How would he react to that occurrence?

5. What steps would he take to solve it?

6. How will he react if he is successful? If he fails?

7. How will he grow and change?

The characters act out, for the reader, the action of the story and the feelings the author wishes to awaken. The characters move about in the setting to give depth and colour, but sometimes it is necessary for the author to play Storyteller.

The characters cannot do all the work themselves. The author must set the scene for them, place them in the action and use transitions to move them through time and space.

THE ENDING

The ending of the story is as important as the beginning. Your reader has struggled through all the characters' trials. He has cried with you and laughed with you and has given his heart to your people. To write a hurried and inferior ending is to cheat him. That is no reward for loyalty!

Every conflict must be resolved logically and in a way that is emotionally satisfying. You want your reader to leave your story feeling you have taken him some place special and introduced him to people he is glad he met—people he will never forget.

You may find you are anxious to tie up all the ends and go on to something new. If you give in to the temptation, your reader is going to feel as if you have pushed him aside.

It's not enough to explain that the detective called everyone into the sitting room and told them the maid killed the master of the house. The reader has to be told why she committed the murder—in a conclusion written to wring the last drop of emotion and suspense.

The same principle applies to romantic fiction. The reader has been through every bit of indecision with the protagonists so it makes sense that he wants to be part of the resolution. One paragraph that states she/he forgave him/her, and they lived happily ever after, is not good enough. The reader wants to be there and experience every emotion.

The resolution to the conflict was plotted before you began. You knew where your characters are going and what they were going to do when they get there. The ending should be a joy to write. Give it the time it deserves.

When you consider your story finished, the need to send it to a publisher the same day will be more than you can stand. Don't do it. Put it away for at least a week. Every writer, no matter how experienced, needs this cooling-off period.

We all fall in love with our work and lose objectivity. Our eye reads what we thought we wrote. We miss typos and contradictions. It is necessary to read printed copy because words look different on paper than they do on the computer screen.

When you take out your manuscript, read it carefully. Look at the characters. Are they alive? Do they jump off the page and talk to you? If not, how can they be brought to life? Look at their motivation. If they are properly motivated, the reader will understand them. If he understands them, he will believe them and they will be real.

Study the dialogue. Does each character have his own voice? Read it aloud. Does it flow? If you stumble, there is something wrong. Rewrite it until you can hear the words in your mind.

Go over the writing. Is it lively and cliche free? Are the chosen nouns the best ones for the job? Are they specific (farmhouse instead of house)? Are the verbs active? (He sauntered is better than he was walking slowly.)

Are the modifiers connected to the correct words or phrases? We all remember high school English and the fun we had with sentences like: The boy ran into the house with the green hat. Of course, the boy, not the house, had the green hat.

Look at the adjectives and adverbs. Have so many been included that they become annoying? Say what you have to say as effectively as possible. Toss out everything that doesn't add to the story.

Punctuation proves to be difficult for many writers. Again, reading the manuscript aloud often shows where commas have been omitted. The dash can make a difference in liveliness and add drama, but take care not to overuse it. Computer grammar-check programmes help if punctuation is a problem.

An important checkpoint is the pace—the rate of development, movement, and progress. The story should seem to move effortlessly, fast enough to ensure reader interest but never so fast that he feels rushed.

If the story seems to be too slow paced, it likely needs to be cut. Editing becomes extremely important. Every word must be examined with the writer asking himself, "Is this necessary to the story?" If not, out it goes, no matter how expressive or artistic the passage might be.

Pace is especially important at the beginning. If the writer explains too much, he forces the story; not enough and there is no hook.

Pace is equally important in the middle of the story. There should not be a string of unrelated events. Events should flow logically, rising one from the other.

Check to see all action follows the rule of cause and effect. Analyze each event in every scene . . . because someone did something, something else happened.

Pace is the most vital at the end of the story. You do not have room to explain every detail, but the resolution has to be complete enough to be satisfying for the reader. Your aim is to make him race toward the climax, anticipating the solution. At the same time, the quality of the writing forces him to savour every word.

The main character reaches a new understanding of the problem. Often, this understanding leads the reader to the theme. The story has said something. Check the symbolism. Does it work? Is it consistent? You can't simply drop something symbolic into a story and leave it there. It has to illustrate a point. Watch how other authors use symbolism, and practise using it. Your stories will have that extra edge all editors seek.

The last thing you must do is examine your own emotional reaction to all aspects of the work. Do you feel sad when the protagonist is sad? Do you smile when he smiles? Do you feel anger, happiness, love... all the emotions you want to bring out in your reader? If you don't have a reaction, your reader won't have one, either.

FINDING IDEAS

Ideas for short stories come from everywhere: personal experience, dreams, newspapers and articles, hobbies, family, pets, children, holidays. You are living in the middle of short story material.

We are told, from the day we express a desire to create, to write what you know. Taken literally, that means writing only what you have lived, but it goes beyond that. It includes all those things you've read about, have observed, and have been told.

We limit ourselves by thinking our ideas must come complete with a compelling plot and fully rounded characters. In reality, the raw material of fiction is an image, a metaphor, a scrap of dialogue from which the plot and the characters grow.

The fewer restrictions we place on ourselves the better the chance of finding a gem that will trigger a remarkable story.

The place you live, and the people you live with, can spark the imagination. Every family has its eccentrics; every neighbourhood, its colourful characters. My gypsy grandmother, and her antics, have been the subject of many pieces of fiction.

The ideas you find in newspapers, magazines, books, or those that come from conversations, present the problem of coming up with something new. It is impossible to tell the whole story. The trick is to find the one thing that will make an event stand out. Usually that is what caught your attention in the first place.

History, fairy tales, myths, all supply ideas that can be fresh if you choose a different point of view. Tell a familiar story through the eyes of a secondary character (who then becomes the protagonist).

Visual images can often lead the writer into a story. Try standing before a painting. Tell what has happened and what is going to happen.

Keep your eyes open when out for a walk. Streets are filled with action and drama. All you have to do is look.

Images you see everyday can trigger a story. What about that cracked vase standing alone on the table, lit by the dim light of a bare bulb. Who owns it? Where did it come from? Why is it there? Inventing questions and answers about an object, starts a story.

Sometimes, a phrase or an isolated bit of dialogue won't leave you alone. Just a few words can be a trigger if you work out the consequences.

Questions we have about people, places, events, even abstract ideas, pressure us into writing. Stories can be built around such topics as: immortality, loneliness, and shadows we turn into reality.

With fiction, the idea lives in language, style, image, point of view, character, and scene. The finished story may be far from the event or image that triggered it.

MARKETS

Book stores and libraries have shelves laden with writers' market material. Take an afternoon and familiarize yourself with what is available because it is here that you will find the best guide to the markets.

Read magazines that publish stories similar to those that interest you. Write to the publishers, requesting their guidelines. Markets and editors are in a constant state of flux so it is important that you keep the guidelines current.

You must know the editorial policy of the publication and the only way you are going to learn that is by studying back issues. There is no point in sending horror fiction to a magazine that publishes nothing but romance.

Initially, it is a good idea to concentrate on a limited number of publications. Read those you like and write to suit their requirements. You have a better chance at selling if you like the subject you are writing!

Start small and work up as you gain publishing credits. Initially, it might be that you are forced to sell for copies only. Fine. The next time you send something out, you can add, I have been published in Today Magazine, and include the tear sheet. The editor doesn't care how much you were paid—he cares that someone else published you.

If the magazines you are thinking of targeting carry stories by three of the country's top writers, forget it until you have an impressive credit sheet. They pay big money for big names.

Don't haggle over price. The first time you are accepted by a publication, prove you can meet deadlines, turn in clean copy, and are pleasant to work with. The next time you submit a piece, they will likely remember you and the sale will be easier. As you become established with an editor, you can invoice along with the submission.

Arrogance has no place in the writing life if you want to sell your work. It takes a long time to get to know the markets, the editors, and to establish a name. The one thing you can be sure of is that every time you sell, you add another publication to your list of credits. It will be that much easier to sell the next thing you write.

CHAPTER EIGHT

SHORT ROMANTIC FICTION

Newsstands and supermarket racks are loaded with what is commonly termed Woman's Fiction. This includes everything from the leading magazines' story of the month to the weeklies that concentrate on "true confession".

The competition is great, but these publications need a steady supply of good fiction to fill their pages. They are looking for love stories: light humorous love stories, serious love stories, love stories that centre around problems and issues.

No matter what the plot and theme, the fiction has one thing in common—the appearance of being true. Female point-of-view is the most popular with editors but it is possible to sell the male-narrator story. It just takes longer.

Your protagonists must be ordinary people in believable situations. The reader accepts that what is happening to the characters could happen to them.

The plot of these stories seems to be simple—more often, it is not. Intelligent characterization brings this fiction to life.

Probably more than in any other market, you write to please the editor and not yourself. The editors know exactly what their readers want and they are astute business people. It is imperative that you are clear about the type of stories the publications are buying. What sells to one, won't necessarily sell to another.

Producing what the editor wants is not as difficult as it might seem. Once you have found a magazine that prints the stories you like to read, analyze each for the following points.

1. The average number of words in each story.

2. The average number of characters.

3. The point of view (voice) used to tell the story.

4. The age group the story targets.

5. The characters' profession.

6. The marital status of most of the characters.

7. The preferred type of ending—happy, hopeful, etc.

8. Are the stories written in first person? Third person? Both? What is the role of the narrator?

9. Are the locations exotic? Local? Mixed?

10. How much editorial space is given to fiction?

You have studied the publication and found the editor prefers stories around 3,000 words, written in first person from the female viewpoint. The protagonist is usually in her mid-thirties, married with a career, and is challenged by internal and external conflicts. The ending is always upbeat.

Now you have the pattern for your story and the starting place for an outline that should include:

1. a brief description of the plot and theme.

2. a list of the characters with a written bio for each.

3. a brief description of the conflict and the resolution.

New writers often have difficulty coming up with a plot because they think they have to produce something that has never been done before—an impossible task. Everything has been done before!

What you are looking for is a new way to tell it. Give the story an unusual theme or write it from a different point-of-view. Use an unexpected location. Give the protagonist a unique way of coping with an ordinary problem.

Your story will stand a better chance of selling if it has a modern theme. "Girl meets-loses-gets boy" fiction will only find a home if the problems are contemporary. They can be an external (job, home, etc.) or internal (passions, fears, etc.), but they must be real conflicts, something with which the reader can identify.

True Confession stories are distinct from other forms of women's fiction. The editors do not demand soaring prose but they do expect good, clear writing with no muddled flashbacks or careless transitions.

Confession stories need more dialogue and make use of extensive detail. Descriptions must be accurate because you are writing "true" stories. If the story is reality based, such as in a medical theme, you must know the symptoms and treatments that will affect the protagonist.

Don't use a problem, no matter how interesting you think it is, if you can't verify the facts to make it ring true. A story focusing on a woman struggling to tell her husband about a cancer diagnosis, requires firsthand knowledge or extensive research.

True confession fiction follows a formula.

1. Start with the character who is going to tell the story. Usually, the female viewpoint is used and it is often told in first person.

2. Give your protagonist a character defect. She can be lazy, jealous, unfaithful, etc. Explain the root of the flaw.

3. Introduce a conflict that has been caused by the character defect.

4. Begin to resolve the problem by having your protagonist make a decision to act. Reveal the results she hopes to obtain from the action.

5. Continue the resolution by making the plan fail. When this happens, the protagonist becomes aware of her character defect and realizes she's largely responsible for her problem.

6. The protagonist begins to make amends and to think of others instead of herself.

7. The protagonist finds happiness, or the hope of happiness, through her sincere attempts to atone for past mistakes.

All these stories are reality based. The author must be aware of changes in social mores, advanced technology and medical breakthroughs. Stories that worked a few years ago, won't work today. For example, it is unlikely that you will sell a story about the shame of an unwanted pregnancy.

The conflicts in women's fiction must reflect the conflicts in life. The issues that concern women today are the bones of your stories, so listen to the people around you. What disturbs women, chatting as they wait, in the supermarket line? What issues are being discussed on radio and television talk shows? What self-help books are selling?

The best plot in the world will fail if the characterization is weak. This kind of fiction demands that you pay attention to detail, make use of in-depth description, and have real characters who "show" what they are doing.

The words your characters use play a major role in their development. If the story you are working on seems sluggish, the way to save it may be through dialogue.

Good dialogue moves your story forward, adds depth, and gives your readers an understanding of the characters. Through conversation you can show what people look like, tell how they are feeling, where they are going, or where they have been.

Dialogue is easier, and more interesting to read, than paragraph after paragraph of narrative. A character who says, "That material is beautiful . . . the dress is so soft. The blue really deepens the blue in your eyes," gives you a lot of information in a few words.

The narrative might read: She wore a blue dress made of a soft material. The colour flattered her because the shade was almost the same as her eyes and deepened the colour.

Good dialogue gives the reader instant information. It sounds natural but it should not be written so authentically that it is punctuated with jargon. Idioms, used sparingly, give the impression of dialect, social status, etc., without annoying the reader.

Sentences, in conversation, are crisp. People talk in phrases and interrupt each other. The exchanges are fast paced and often show the nature of the speaker.

A long string of information should be handled in shared dialogue between characters. Identification words, John said, Jane asked quietly, help the reader to know who is talking and the mood of the speaker.

Add little gestures that make the character more vivid. Maybe she has a habit of running her fingers through her hair when she's nervous. Maybe he strokes his chin or frowns when he's deep in thought.

Remember, these gestures and expressions of mood are written with tag words. They are not used as tag words. You cannot say, "I saw you," John laughed. John did not laugh the words—he said them. The correct sentence would be: "I saw you," John said with a laugh.

When you have written the dialogue, make sure it serves a purpose. It should give some information about the speaker, show his emotional state, or move the story forward.

Read it aloud. Does it flow? Is there enough reader identification? Too much? Do the tag words follow the tone of the scene?

Dialogue is an important tool for showing emotion. In a few words, you can bring to life the state of each character. In short romance fiction, emotion is a key ingredient for success. This is escapist fiction. It is not meant to tax the mind or to leave the reader feeling life is an unending struggle.

Readers and editors want a happy resolution with all the loose ends neatly tied. This is not the genre for unexplained characters, surprise endings, or sadness.

WHERE TO FIND IDEAS

Look around you. Listen to everything. Find the dreams and desires of real people and you have the theme and plot for your story. Draw on personal experience. If something has happened that made an impact on your life, you have the base for strong reader identification and, therefore, successful fiction.

Read advice and opinion columns. Study the human interest stories in newspapers and magazines, and fictionalize them. Television, books and even book titles will trigger ideas or spark a memory that can be developed into a plot.

The key to this market is finding an idea with strong, romantic appeal. Never lose sight of what you are writing—and why. This is "feel good fiction" with an uncomplicated message.

MARKETS

Almost without exception, magazines carry at least one piece of fiction in each issue. The more fiction it carries, the better your chance of selling to the publication.

Every magazine has editorial requirements that differ from all the others. It is imperative that you write for the guidelines before you submit a manuscript.

Reading back issues will give you an idea of which magazines you want to write for—they should be the ones you enjoy. Start with three or four and tailor your material to their editorial specifications.

As you sell to one, add another until you become familiar with what the market has to offer. If you try to absorb all of the periodicals at once, you will find yourself feeling defeated before you start.

Be realistic. Don't aim for the top-selling magazines until you have a substantial credit list. Give yourself every chance for success.

Writers' market publications carry detailed lists of potential magazines, catalogued by category. These are usually titled: Confession, General Interest, Women's.

Payment increases with the prestige of the publication. While you are establishing credits, you may sell for as little as ten cents a word—perhaps, even for copies.

Each time a submission is accepted, you are a step closer to being bumped into the higher paying markets. Some larger houses pay as much as two dollars a word. Some pay a flat-rate that can run $3500 for 2000 words. Longer manuscripts can earn even more.

This is a lucrative market and one of the best places for a new writer to break into the business.

CHAPTER NINE

WRITING THE MYSTERY

The mystery story had its roots in the fifteenth century morality play, created to call attention to transgression. The difference in today's mystery is that it mirrors the lawlessness of this century but it does not focus only on the seven deadly sins. Modern culprits work within the framework of felonies committed against society, and punishment goes beyond social condemnation.

Part of reader satisfaction comes from the pleasure found in unravelling crimes and unveiling criminals. As people, we live comfortably within a code of ethics where wrongdoing is recognized as a hostile act. The mental role we, as readers, play in correcting antisocial behaviour gives us a great deal of enjoyment.

Mystery writers use devices that entertain: villains of superior intelligence, eerie and exotic settings, fast-paced dialogue, and engrossing heros and heroines. They use intricately woven plots, well-placed clues, and startling resolutions.

Plot unity, so important, often depends on unity in the author's mood. Ideally, the first draft is written in one sitting; therefore, outlines, character biographies, and careful structuring are vital. These stories must know where they are going before you start to write.

Mystery is not an easy genre. The guidelines are strict. Essentially, these are stories of action with a theme, and must work towards the resolution of that theme. Action is introduced quickly, the progression to the conclusion is logical, and the solution is unexpected but believable.

Characters are consistent in their attitudes and actions. They are more important for what they do than for who they are. While their actions do result from who they are, those actions must always fit the theme of the story.

Setting, too, is tailored to fit the theme that can be broken down into two elements: the choice of the crime and the author's attitude toward the crime. The writer's attitudes (personal views) are most dramatically represented in this genre and will affect the outcome of the story.

HOW TO WRITE

A factual world is created by getting material from the real world. The story may be fiction but things like gun calibre, symptoms of poisons, and forensic and court detail, are authentic. If you are sure of your facts, the reader will sense that assurance, and the plot becomes believable.

The accomplished writer takes seemingly expendable data and ties it in with the plot as a form of dropping clues. However, all the information he uses must serve to move the story. Unlike the novel, the short mystery does not allow time for wandering or developing scenes purely for entertainment.

Environment creates feelings that give the story its tone and mood. Finding the victim in a setting that evokes strong feelings, helps to set that tone. Pulling a body from the sea brings on a different reaction than from finding a body crammed into the trunk of a car.

Many new writers think that because mysteries are fun to read, they are easy to write. They choose their crime, develop suspects and sleuths, build motives and throw in subterfuge, but the story doesn't work. What is missing is the certainty of cause and effect—the force behind the mystery.

The cause is desperation and the effect is disaster. The writer persuades the reader of the gravity of the situation and the importance of making it right. He directs the reader's attention to the facts and impressions that deal directly with the crime and its solution.

The motives must be strong and the gimmicks used, meaningful. Characters are never introduced at random and they do not disappear without having accomplished a purpose. Information is not added because you are proud of your knowledge. Everything irrelevant lessens the power of the story.

Cause is the reason for the story (the crime). It is the idea. Effect, how the story develops, is the plot. The plot comes alive and becomes the story when you introduce characters who cause events that effect them.

The time of the crime is stressed because it is the link to the alibi. Through the alibi, you add other suspects that create doubt in the reader's mind. You must link the other suspects convincing to each other and to the protagonist. Clues point to each suspect, and everything takes place within a solid setting.

Plot the story mentally before you write a detailed outline. You can begin with a character, a setting, a crime—anything that leaps out and starts your imagination.

Mystery stories do not allow you the luxury of discovering the plot, while you work, as mainstream fiction sometimes does. You must know the cause and effect of your crime and understand the motivation of each character involved.

Before you start to write, you have a grasp on the beginning, the middle and the end. You have made time charts that plot the sequence of events and the placement of the characters within the story. You fully understand that your story is the events that happen . . . the raw material. . . . and the plot is the structure that you impose on those events.

Shaping your plot, from the raw material, involves the following steps. I have used a murder for simplicity.

1. The killer meets the victim and an exchange takes place.

2. The killer murders the victim.

3. The murder is discovered and the detective enters the case.

4. An investigation follows.

5. The detective solves the murder.

6. The killer is apprehended.

This is a good place for a novice writer to begin. The pattern can be adapted to other crimes. As you become comfortable with the genre, you'll find you are exploring and expanding the format.

The steps can be ordered to suit the story you are writing. It can be told in a linear fashion, starting at step one and working through the events as they occur.

The steps can be rearranged so that you start with the murder, mask the identity of the killer, and follow the detective through the investigation. You may start with the murder, reveal the identity of the killer, and watch the detective work toward the resolution.

You may start with the discovery of the murder, call in the detective, and throw out clues to mask the identity of the killer. There are many ways of arranging these six steps, each as effective as the other.

The Plot Wheel has long been a favourite tool of the fiction writer and is one of the best ways for a novice to learn structure. For example, in the centre, the hub, is the crime. From the crime, the spokes of the wheel form a radial graph of information.

At twelve o'clock is a spoke labelled, the scene of the crime. The branches from this spoke carry the subheadings: place, body, weapon, clues.

Moving clockwise, the next spoke is the victim, with the branches, who he is and why he was murdered. Background follows with subheadings: character background, local background and setting.

The next spoke is suspects, with the branches: motives, opportunities, links to the victim.

The next, time graph, has: when the crime took place, whereabouts of the suspects, the time element of the story (days, weeks).

Choose the point of view for the next spoke. Add: first person, third person, narrator, multiple viewpoint, in the branches.

Secondary characters divide: purpose to the story, information supplied.

The detective or investigator has the next spoke divided into: who, why

The criminal follows with: who, motive.

The final spoke is the solution. It separates into the detective, the clues and the criminal.

Draw the wheel on a large piece of heavy paper, label the spokes and their branches, and tack it to the wall. You can start your story at any spoke, follow it clockwise, and the plot construction emerges.

Let's look at a crime, following the radial graph. We'll use murder again, for simplicity, but the wheel will work for any offense.

THE CRIME = MURDER

1. The first spoke = the SCENE OF THE CRIME.

Place: Stewart Jordon's (the victim) office.

Body: the victim was at the scene of the crime.

Weapon: a small calibre hand gun.

Clue: the papers in his desk and in the filing cabinet are strewn about. The safe was open. There were signs of a struggle. Nothing was taken.

2. Next, THE VICTIM.

Who: Stewart Jordon, CEO of Jordon Imports, a company that brings in product from Asia. A multi-millionaire, he has lived on the edge and made many enemies. He is 48, married with two grown sons who have nothing to do with the business. He has always had a mistress. His wife is a "show piece", his lovers are entertainment and his business associates are expendable in his eyes.

Why: He was hated by his rivals because he stops at nothing to get what he wants. He was hated by his wife because of his affairs and his treatment of his children, and he was hated by his ex-lovers.

3. BACKGROUND.

Character's background is done in bios. Local background and settings: Stewart's office in Rockland Heights, Stewart's and Bill's home, both in the Uplands, Jane and Ed's home in the suburbs, and Charlie's apartment in town. The Story is set in Vancouver, B.C. Details of locations are done as part of the bio.

4. SUSPECTS with motives, opportunity, and links to the victim.

Bill—a business partner who was in constant conflict with Stewart. He stayed late at work that night.

Jane—the victim's secretary who was, until recently, his lover. She left the office after Stewart fired her but she returned, wanting to talk to him. She was seen reentering. She finds the body.

Ed—Jane's husband, who found out about the affair. He told a friend he was going to confront the victim and make him pay for ruining his life.

Charlie—right-hand man of a corporate player, Davidson Kimber, who is known for his ruthlessness in takeovers. Kimber has been trying to take Stewart's company. Charlie was seen entering the building but no one saw him leave.

5. TIME GRAPH

When the crime took place: after 6 P.M. but before 8 P.M. when Jane found the body.

Whereabouts of the suspects:

Bill said he left shortly before 7 P.M. but a security guard saw him at 7:30 P.M..

Jane claims she was making night deposits, came back to the office to pick up some papers before she went home, and found the body.

Ed claims he was home but he was seen by a neighbour at 8 P.M.. When questioned he said he had gone for a walk.

Charlie says he was out of town but can't prove it.

Time element of the story.

The murder, investigation and resolution take place over a two-week period.

6. POINT-OF-VIEW

The story is told in third person with narrator (author's) voice for transitions and some descriptions. The detective is the protagonist. Everything is from his point-of-view.

7. SECONDARY CHARACTERS.

a) Each suspect.

b) Gary, a confidant of the detective (protagonist), used to reveal clues and to show the progression of the investigation through dialogue.

c) Nancy, the detective's wife, is used to show the personality of the protagonist, and to reveal story progression and clues that puzzle her husband.

8. THE DETECTIVE

The key character in the story. He is 35, married but has no children—a conscious decision. He is obsessed with his job, often at the expense of friends and family, but he is close to his wife and respected by colleagues. He is particularly interested in this murder because he suspects corruption in the victim's business connections and operations. He sees the investigation going beyond the actual crime.

9. THE CRIMINAL

Who: Jane.

Why: The motive is revenge. Jane doesn't accept any responsibility for her actions, but blames all of her problems, at home and at work, on Stewart. She is obsessed with him, her aim is to be his wife, and she refuses to let go. When he fires her after several attempts to end the relationship, she won't accept it. Jane doesn't tell anyone she lost her job. She returns to the office to beg him to take her back. Jane carries a small hand gun for protection because she made night deposits, often worked late and was on the streets alone. When Stewart won't talk to her, she flies into a rage. There is a struggle, she pulls the gun, and kills him. When she realizes she can't get out of the building without being seen, she fakes a robbery and then pretends to find the body.

10. THE SOLUTION

From the detective's point of view: the investigation is charted from the finding of the body, the suspects' interviews, the clues, and the motivation and opportunity.

The clues are explained and show the reader how they lead the detective to the criminal.

The criminal's reaction is recorded. He can respond with violence or acceptance. His punishment, or an indication of the punishment, is revealed.

Every story has a beginning, a middle and an end. The beginning is the introduction, the middle is the elaboration, and the ending is the conclusion.

The mystery follows a basic profile.

1. THE BEGINNING

a) Introduce the victim and the criminal.

b) Bring in the murder and the clues.

c) Introduce who finds the body.

d) Introduce the investigator.

2. THE MIDDLE

a) Development of the suspects.

b) Interrogation of the suspects.

c) Development of the clues.

d) Introduction of the subplot. This includes love interests, family conflict, fighting addictions.

e) Begin to eliminate suspects.

3.THE END

a) Close in on the criminal.

b) Confrontation of criminal.

c) Apprehending the criminal.

d) Explain clues kept from the reader.

e) Resolve murder.

f) Resolve subplots.

The opening is the most important part of the story. To be a true mystery, there must be a puzzle to solve. Your reader needs to know what that is and to take the first steps toward a solution in the first paragraphs of the story.

There must be a narrative hook to grab the reader and immediately involve him in the action. This is accomplished by beginning the suspense in the first paragraph.

The climax is the next most important part of the story. Good stories can be destroyed by disappearing characters, unexplained clues, or long-winded explanations given after the action is completed. Save something exciting for the very last page.

Keep the story moving. Make every word count. If a character or an action doesn't move the plot forward, take it out. You may complicate a problem with coincidence (bad luck, natural disaster, accident) but you are advised not to solve it by any means other than through the actions of the protagonist.

The protagonist must answer all of the questions in a realistic, logical way. A strong protagonist, one who evokes reader sympathy, can lead to series characters. If something has worked well, consider using it again. Many successful mystery writers base much of their work around one detective.

WHERE TO FIND IDEAS

Finding ideas is like searching for clues. You'll never be without a notebook because you will discover storylines in almost everything you do and wherever you go.

Personal experience can lead to interesting plots. Visit a court house and observe the trials. Sit in the waiting room of a hospital. Talk to members of your local police force. Newspapers, books, book titles, television, all trigger ideas.

A person's peculiarities can inspire an idea for a victim. What about the neighbour who refuses to lock the doors, or one who willingly picks up hitchhikers? Have you worked for an aggressive boss? Dealt with a possessive or obsessive personality? If so, you have ready made ideas for victims and criminals.

Places can also evoke ideas. Visiting an old mansion can spark the imagination and bring to life a story about murder in the castle. A deserted street can lead to a mugging or rape. Hazardous sites (balconies, derelict boats, subways, parks at night) that bring out uncomfortable emotions in you will draw the same emotions from your reader.

Once you have an idea, start collecting material. Build a file that contains newspaper clippings, magazine profiles, notes of conversations or observations—anything that has to do with the plot and theme.

While the file is expanding, the story will be hardening in your mind. When you begin to write, your research will be completed, the idea solidly formed, and the words will begin to flow.

MARKETS

Every writer's market publication contains submission information. Many magazines are devoted entirely to the mystery genre. Each follows a particular editorial requirement so it is imperative that you write for their guidelines.

This is a lucrative market, with many periodicals buying short mystery when they are buying nothing else. Submarkets exist: romantic suspense, paranormal

suspense, young adult adventure/mystery. If your story has a timeless quality, and is well-written, it will likely find a home.

CHAPTER TEN
WRITING SCIENCE FICTION

The term science fiction loosely applies to several categories of fiction. "Science fiction" and "speculative fiction" are viewed as the same by most writers and editors, and are often called SF or sci-fi.

"Fantasy" is a general term for any fictional work that is not devoted to literal portrayal of the known world. It is often coupled with science fiction but it is a separate category.

"Space opera," the material produced for cheaper, mass-market publications, is filled with brawny villains rescuing lusty princesses from the clutches of Zeegog, Ruler of Hyperspace—or something equally far-fetched.

Space opera is not science fiction at all. It borrows techniques and tricks, is imitative, but fails to explore the human condition that is a trademark of real science fiction.

A science fiction story starts with an act of the mind, moves from is to if, and is always logical. The imagination is controlled by the intellect. It becomes reality through ideas and has a rational reason for everything that happens.

This genre is not a leap into the impossible but a discipline that accepts science and respects the way it arrives at fact. SF makes its connection with the reader through reality of ideas. It is speculation of the thinking mind.

Events make sense within the cause and effect system. While these events can be imaginative, they cannot happen simply because the author wishes them to happen. How and why, asked at any point in the story, should be able to be answered.

Nothing ever occurs that contradicts what is known to be known. For example, the authentic science fiction story would not have a 300-foot man roaming the earth. Gravity alone would make him crumble. It would be impossible for him to exist.

Science fiction starts with a known fact, tries not to contradict what is known, and plays with where, why, what, if.

Fantasy, on the other hand, makes its connection through emotions rather than logic. It relies heavily on ordinary physical perception and lets things happen because they "feel right" to the author.

Unlike SF, fantasy characters can do anything they want and events can take place at the writer's whim. The 300-foot man could exist without anyone giving a thought—or an explanation—to such trivial detail as gravity. The basic element in fantasy is: something rationally unexplainable.

Fantasy and science fiction sometimes overlap but it is best to keep them separate. Many elements in fantasy are disturbing in a science fiction story, and vice versa. The ending that is satisfactory for one will not be for the other. Characters cannot be interchanged and settings are different. Mix the two categories and you will frustrate your reader.

HOW TO WRITE

There are five basic techniques that science fiction writers need to develop.

1. Strong characters within the genre. Most fiction succeeds or fails on the strength of its characters. Readers identify with solid, well-rounded persona in mainstream fiction—science fiction is no different.

There are SF stories in which the characters play a role secondary to the scientific or political idea that inspired them but they are usually "trick" stories and seldom remembered. The best science fiction has absorbing characters who struggle to solve their problems, the same as any other fiction.

2. Speculation. Many science fiction stories are triggered when the author starts asking "what if..."

What if UFOs landed on earth?

What if World War II had not occurred?

What if we have another Ice Age?

At first, it may seem that speculation opposes realism because it takes a blind leap into the unknown, but it is necessary if you are going to write a good science fiction story. If you use only carefully researched facts, your story will be dull and predictable.

Extrapolation, a carefully worked out step into the future, can go hand in hand with speculation. It begins by asking if questions:

If we build "thinking" computers and give them free will, what will happen?

If DNA splicing is used in humans, what will happen to life as we know it?

If we find life on other planets . . . and so on.

Each question could inspire valid science fiction. Many successful stories were started in a contemporary setting with something added to change the scene: a deadly virus, a time machine, a space invasion, a mutation.

Speculation is important to science fiction but it must be informed speculation, not simply wild flights of imagination.

3. Projection. This is one of the first gimmicks used by writers of science fiction. The author takes a chapter from history, projects it into the future, and sets his imagination free. The advantage of using a historical event is that you have a solid sense of character and plot before you start to write.

Anything can inspire you. For example, the Russian Revolution, the people and the circumstance, can be projected into a futuristic setting, or the conquests of the great explorers can be played out in an interstellar setting.

4. Consistency. Every story you write must be consistent, each part working together to produce a unified, believable whole. You can't have a bathing beauty romping in the surf on Mars any more than you can solve your hero's problems by having him make three wishes.

Every part of the story must lead smoothly to the next. The factors must reinforce each other and work together to produce a story that is internally consistent if you are to maintain your reader's trust and expectation of belief.

5. Research. I have heard new writers say they like science fiction because they are free to let their imagination wander . . . they can do as they please without having to worry about researching facts. That might be true for space opera, even fantasy, but it is not true for science fiction.

No writer can know enough to build a realistic story entirely out of his imagination. Research is vital to realism. Remember, you are dealing with science fiction so if you are setting your story on Venus, you'd better know something about the place.

Imagination and information interact: a fact will suggest a story, an idea will demand a check to see if the fact is valid, and the writer's mind puts everything together.

Facts and logic often stimulate the imagination because things are more interesting when you know what can and cannot be done. A well-planned, extra-terrestrial world has a lot more surprises in it than a mere copy of planet earth.

Environments, sociologies, histories, languages, must be researched and projected into the extrasolar world of your imagination.

BACKGROUND

Most science fiction takes place in the future so the background is largely part of the writer's imagination. Once you have researched the known, conjecture begins to build the world.

Structuring story background for the near future (twenty to fifty years from now) is often more difficult than creating an alien planet in some distant age.

Working with near future, the writer cannot depend wholly on his imagination. Extensive research must be conducted to reveal what scientists and engineers project for future life. Extrapolation makes a logical world possible. Characters are similar to the people of today.

In far future, the author has more freedom to create bizarre cultures. You rely less on research and more on imagination. No one knows what life will be like 2000 years from now. No scientist or engineer can make a valid prediction about how the world will be structured.

The only rule for far future stories is that your background must be consistent in its details.

Success lies in how well you feature your imaginary world. If you are vague, no one will believe your concept. When constructing background, consider the following points:

1. MORAL CODES. You must assume that morality will change. You cannot construct conflict and resolution within your own moral guidelines. Remember, in the 1940s and 50s, no one would have believed that in twenty years, "free love" would be acceptable.

The future has infinite possibilities. When building your society, consider the moral questions in context with those of today. For example: how will murder be viewed? What about euthanasia? Killings done in the name of service to one's country?

Listing the questions that will be included in your story often helps with their projection into the future.

2. DOMESTIC POLITICS. The political structure of your country must be examined. For example, will Canadian parliament work as it does today? Will there be two major

parties in the United States elections? What about democracy? Will war still be an issue?

3. WORLD POLITICS. There have been major changes to the world scene in a few years. Many stories that were constructed even recently have lost their validity. What can happen over the next fifty years? Will Canada still exist? Will the United States? How will world power be divided?

4. DAILY LIVING. This is one of the most important background elements in your futuristic setting. Your story may be based on morality, politics or religion, but it is the detail about day-to-day life that is going to make your story believable.

The problems of today—pollution, population explosion, poverty, disease—will be the basis of the issues of tomorrow. Family life, homes, the work place, all must be projected into the future. The trick lies with changing them.

How will the citizens of tomorrow dress? What form of transportation will they use? Will everything be done by computer? What foods will they eat? How will it be prepared?

The questions go on forever and you need the answers if you are going to write an effective science fiction story. You must know your futuristic setting as well as you know your world today.

PLOTTING

When plotting your science fiction story, you must be sure that all ingredients mesh into a rational whole. For example, if you extrapolate a future Canada run by a dictatorship, you must not portray a society where the arts flourish—rarely have the two coexisted.

Plotting isn't mechanical. People and circumstances affect each other. The same rules that apply in mainstream fiction, apply in science fiction. Outlines are written, character bios are done, and you know where you're going before you begin to write. Preplanning prevents factual errors or contradictions in logic.

As in mainstream, there will be surprises along the way. A character's believable action will change the storyline. Cause and effect come into play.

The plot is not a mass of researched, technical knowledge but an attitude toward the knowledge. Curiosity is the attitude of those who write, and read, science fiction.

CHARACTERIZATION

The best way to make a story realistic is to people it with realistic characters. You can pattern them after people you know even in science fiction. As you write, they will take on personalities of their own.

In science fiction the characters are not always human beings. They are anything with an intelligence: robots, computers, aliens—even mutated animals and fish.

However, every one of them has human traits because these are the qualities with which the reader can identify. Each character, no matter how they look, must experience human problems and present some human emotion—love, loyalty, humour, courage.

Biographies for the characters are extremely important. It is easier to lose track of a horned, orange-skinned, green-haired, alien than it is the humans of mainstream. But, how do you create a believable alien?

Building an alien character is difficult. It takes much thought and planning to design physical characteristics, environment, language and emotional involvement. You want to avoid creating an alien shell—a human in a creature suit.

Science fiction readers are a demanding audience. They make a game of finding all the author's science errors, forcing him to establish every detail of the story. If your plot needs an alien, then consider the following points for making him believable.

1. ANATOMY

Should your alien be male or female? Perhaps you need to develop a third sex. How many legs does he need to walk in his world? How many arms does he need? How are the eyes positioned? Are the ears external? How would he evolve under the scientific conditions on his planet?

Don't be limited by what looks familiar on earth. Anything that can be explained as a logical evolutionary development is reasonable.

2. PSYCHOLOGY

The science of nature, functions, and phenomena plays an important part in all science fiction writing. For example, gravity. On a heavy gravity planet, a drop of only a few feet would prove fatal. The alien would fear heights. On a planet with near-zero gravity, free flight could be part of everyday life.

3. PHYSICS

Science fiction is sometimes classified as hard, referring to the degree of science connected with it. For example, if there is a lot of mathematics involved in proving the premise, the writing is said to be "hard."

Unless you have a scientific background, you might want to avoid these subjects. It is difficult to detail an alien living on a neutron star unless you have a working knowledge of matter and anti-matter.

Write within the realm of your understanding. You can effectively describe a strange environment, play with the development of a culture, and create wondrous aliens by using physics familiar to you.

4. BIOCHEMISTRY

What is the basic body biochemistry of the alien? What does he breathe? What are the limits of livable body temperature? If you choose a different chemical basis for life, keep in mind that your alien couldn't share our environment. Also, be sure that what you have chosen is theoretically possible.

5. CULTURE

Culture and personality are likely the most important part of alien characterization. You have created a background, given descriptions of environment, anatomy and biochemistry. Now you must develop true feeling for your character and the culture in which he lives.

Questions about language arise. Will he be able to learn English? Does he use a mechanical decoding device? You will need to invent a few words of alien language for use in basic communication but don't overdo it.

Consideration must be given to body language because it is a set of visual codes. As a writer, you cannot take the easy way out and let your alien nod his head yes and no. Human body language won't do. Any gestures he makes will have to be explained.

Your creature may appear strange to human eyes, but looks alone do not create an alien being. You need a touch of intellectual and emotional "strangeness," evolution, and the culture that created him.

You need to understand the events that trigger your creature's responses. Once this happens, you will have the alien interacting with you in action and dialogue. He will do what any character in any other form of fiction does—take over the story.

Appearance, gestures, habits, expressions, actions and reactions all help to make a nonhuman real. The writer rounds out the character by giving him a manner of dress, moral codes, living habits, social custom, religion—every facet of his daily life.

If more than one alien appears in the story, you must make sure they are unlike each other, the same way as any human being is unlike his neighbour. They will share attitudes and reactions, as a species, but opinions and personalities will differ.

FINDING IDEAS.

Every science fiction writer is plagued with the question, Where do you get those crazy ideas? Getting ideas is seldom a problem.

Perhaps the best source is science itself. Newspapers, and magazines catering to scientific premise, are filled with potential storylines. History can readily be adapted. So can literature, politics, war, religion, and social theory.

It is important that you read. And read! You cannot write this genre if you don't read and enjoy it.

Subscriptions to science news publications help keep you up-to-date with advancements and discoveries.

Encyclopedias are a treasure trove of ideas. Texts are written about every scientific subject and are available at the library. Librarians are glad to help writers track things down.

Professionals are often willing to meet with writers seeking information. Phone and make an appointment, and plan your questions in advance.

Ideas are all around you. Start a file for plotlines, aliens, and background. Keep a notebook. The more you look for ideas, the more you will find.

MARKETS.

Science fiction has a large following and many publications concentrate on the genre. These are listed in writer's market material. Write for the guidelines. Newsletters focus on current topics and up-to-date market information. They are available by subscription.

Conventions are part of the science fiction world and provide valuable access to the marketplace. Editors, writers and agents attend these gatherings.

Keep in mind that real science fiction is fiction about human beings dealing with science or technology.

CHAPTER ELEVEN

WRITING WESTERNS

The Traditional Western story occurs sometime between the American Civil War and the 1890s, which is about the time the frontier vanished. These Westerns focus on loners in armed conflict—for example, the young rancher, struggling to carve out his niche while fighting off the corrupt cattle baron.

Very few traditional Western heros are married and women, when they appear, are on the periphery of the story. While love is not strictly forbidden, there is generally no significant romantic interest. Emotions are largely restricted. Heros are poker-faced and dispassionate men who avoid anything resembling laughter, anger, tenderness or shame.

A traditional, or "formula," Western is rigidly structured and any writer who breaks the rules will not get his work published. Simplicity and violent action are the reference points, with one theme, justice, fundamental to the plot. There are variations but they all deal with the righting of wrongs.

Westerns are also written about the historic west. These stories abandon formula and are free to create a gallery of offbeat characters and interesting plotlines.

The historic west, as opposed to the mythic or traditional west, is an inspiring area for the writer. He can abandon the confines of the traditional Western and explore the forbidden regions of humour and sex. He can tackle whatever wilderness he chooses, and place his hero in any situation, but he must never forget he is the reader's only guide.

Research is mandatory for historical westerns and it must be done long before the writing begins. If the author chooses turn-of-the-century Midwest as his setting, he'd better understand the people, the place and the politics. He must know everything from railroad timetables to medical practices.

The writer must acquire a feel for the lives of the ordinary people, the prejudices of the time, the dreams and the scams. He must know about the newspapers and the books; the clothing and the meals.

HOW TO WRITE

A convention of the classic western is that strong characters are shown only in the depiction of action. The reader is never made aware of the hero's tribulation or indecision, his dreams, desires, or jubilation. The one important thing is the flow of action.

These heros are born leaders who never experience dissension within the ranks of their allies and who enjoy dominating women. They are single, rootless and avoid being drawn into unnecessary conflict. They are shy about their skills, a trait that contrasts dramatically with the villains' display of sadism, greed, and lust.

The beginning of the traditional Western tells the reader who wants what and why it is out of reach. Evil must appear to be winning.

The middle of the story shifts the reader's interest to who is doing what to whom, and how long they can tolerate it.

The end is predictable but no one knows how it will be accomplished. Here lies the suspense. The climax comes only after the action has peaked and the hero has been challenged. His friends, doubting his courage, are relieved to find that what they suspected all along is true—the hero shoots back when provoked, even if he's outnumbered.

Secondary characters follow rules as well. Wives and daughters are chaste. Dance hall girls are promiscuous but never vindictive. The town drunk, or another non-threatening character, can betray the hero out of fear or weakness but never out of greed. That's saved for the villain.

Action, not opinion, moves the traditional Western. Dialogue is used only to supplement that action. The format is visual, not verbal.

Prose is meaty, fast-paced and tough, but it has direction and control. Passive voice, compound verbs, dependent clauses and stylistic tricks have no place in this writing. The formula Western is a study of universal justice, with virtue forever triumphant over evil.

The author who wants to break the rules and create a kindly cattle baron, a soft-hearted thief, or a hero with complicated character defects, can do so by writing a historical Western. However, he does so at some risk.

What he is attempting challenges the Western myth and, if he fails, the reader will not forgive him. In reality, the west was a menacing, desolate place, riddled with disease, violence and corruption.

The comforts of civilization were unavailable for those people not living along railroad lines. Few towns had plumbing, water, or public transportation. Dirt and danger were everywhere.

The writer is faced with the challenge of telling a story about real people in a real time. The hero has ordinary courage and is living with character defects. He changes—for good or for bad—by the end of the story.

The historical west offers material for more colourful and dramatic settings than those used in the traditional Western. There has never been anything like this unique period and there never will be again. It gives the writer a chance to draw from vivid action and interesting people.

New writers often make the mistake of using stereotypical dialect when creating western dialogue. The expressions one associates with the "old west" are strung like beads across the page. While the characters do need to have their own voice, idioms should be used sparingly and only to give the flavour of the times.

Violence is the stuff of drama and popular with readers of Westerns, but writers should use it only in ways that are comfortable to them and natural to the story. When used gratuitously, the work suffers. A western hero, who has a little humanity about him, is not a hero the reader will accept.

IDEAS.

Read the genre! There is no other way to fully understand the concept of western writing. Once you see the patterns and can work easily with them, you will find ideas everywhere.

Television, movies, books and magazine stories will trigger ideas for you. History is a major source for traditional and historical Westerns. Keep a notebook and jot down those things that come to mind. If you don't, you will forget them before you get a chance to write your story.

MARKETS

The best advice I can give you is to stick to the traditional Western when trying to break into the field. Follow the rules and submit to the publications that specialize in the genre. These are listed in writers' market material.

Once you have established a list of publishing credits you can branch out to the historical Western. Read the publications doing these stories so that you are familiar with the editorial policy of each. Write for the guidelines, read back issues, and try to find an angle that makes your writing distinctive.

In spite of the recent reduction of several western lines, the genre is not in danger of vanishing. The upheaval in the market is presenting an opportunity for writers to experiment with new forms of fiction. Formulas may one day be forgotten, opening new areas of interest to the creative mind.

Serialized stories are being enjoyed by people in all walks of life. Publishers are leaning toward the historical Westerns so any writer willing to research and write about the real frontier, with realistic heros and plotlines, can capture a piece of the market.

CHAPTER TWELVE
WRITING FOR CHILDREN

The preschool to young adult market is probably the most misunderstood of any today. Writers browse through children's books and stories, become convinced they can produce something as good in a matter of hours, and then can't understand why their work doesn't sell.

Writing for children is truly a labour of love and the people who know this are successful in the field. It is impossible to effectively write something because you believe it to be "in demand" or think it will make a lot of money.

You write because the subject fits your interest and ability. You touch the child within and, in doing so, it becomes possible for you to touch your reader. Children are tough critics. They will not continue to read a story that starts slowly. They will not tolerate inconsistent characters or tedious dialogue. If they don't like the beginning, they simply put it down and walk away.

Children read for many reasons. They read to learn, to enjoy the familiar and to explore the unknown. They read to laugh and to dream. Each time a child encounters a piece of literature, he is changed by the experience. He sees the world in a different way.

There is an astounding assortment of material that is labelled children's literature. There are picture books, with and without text; easy-to-read books for the beginning reader; pop-up books and adventure books. There is poetry, legend, myth and fantasy; historical fiction, science fiction, mystery and animal stories. Some literature gives children a better understanding of their world. Some prepares them for the future. All of it entertains.

Until the twentieth century, children's literature was not taken seriously enough to demand a place in the publishing world. Today, books written for children have advanced to reflect their intellectual ability, their condition of life, racial heritage, and moral standards.

The changes in society's standards are reflected in the writing, making the stories more accurate and candid than they were even a few years ago. Fiction finds focus in such topics as children's rights, environmental concerns, the plight of the disabled, poverty and death.

Editors are anxious to produce the best possible product but they also know that product must sell. No house can afford to take chances with books or stories that have no hope of attaining a reasonable profit margin. They search for the manuscript with unusual qualities.

HOW TO WRITE

Good storytellers do not imitate another writer's style. They are aware of their own limitations and do not attempt to tell stories that are beyond them. They are cautious about narrative from other cultures, especially if it requires the use of dialect.

The storyteller needs to know his audience—the age and experience—before he selects a topic. Once the writer has found the plot and theme, the next step is to find a starting place.

Some writers plan the entire story beforehand. Other have a rough outline, discovering the plot twists and resolutions as they go. Still others start with a character or a situation.

My advice is, have an outline to give you direction, even if you find you are changing it as you move forward. Designing your plot ensures a good beginning that leads smoothly to the middle, and then to an ending that is the logical outcome of everything that has gone before.

Children's stories are often inspired by an endearing character who is used repeatedly with great success. Pooh

Bear is the example that comes to mind. The character is placed in a situation new to him and the writer recounts what develops, sometimes without knowing exactly where it will end.

When the story is inspired by an incident, the author is usually sure of the ending. He builds the characters to react to an event within the child's realm of knowledge and experience.

STRUCTURE

1. PLOT

All stories start with an idea that falls into three categories: a quest, virtue conquers all, and the growth of the protagonist when faced with a moral dilemma.

2. BEGINNING

a) Give the reader enough information to identify the storyline. (Animal, family, friendship)

b) Tell the reader something about the character. (Name, age, kind of animal)

c) Identify the setting. (House, yard, imaginary place)

d) Move into the action in a way that is interesting to the reader. Present questions that will make him continue reading to find the answers. Don't squeeze too much information into the beginning. Include only what he needs to know and save the rest for later.

3. MIDDLE.

a) Keep your focus.

b) Move the story logically toward the end.

c) Keep the action moving.

d) Give the protagonist problems to overcome and the tools with which to conquer them.

4. END

a) Know what the solution is going to be.

b) Know the growth of the protagonist.

c) Be sure the ending is appropriate and logical for the action.

d) A happy ending is important when writing for young children or for traditional stories, such as fables. Other forms of stories may have varied endings.

5. DIALOGUE.

When writing for children, pay attention to the dialogue. The reader must know who is speaking. Each character has his own voice and speaks in realistic patterns.

Be sure the dialogue is appropriate for the age of the child and the speakers involved. Keep all conversation short and don't let your characters' dialogue hold up the action.

Keep in mind the following points as you begin to structure your story:

a) Don't try to write for children because you think it's easier than writing for adults.

b) Don't underestimate your readers' intelligence.

c) Don't "write down" to children. If you hook your reader, he will make an effort to understand the vocabulary you have chosen.

d) Don't shy away from complex issues. You don't always have to create worlds that are safe and cosy.

c) Show the reader the action by revealing it through the key character's eyes. Experiment with this and other forms until you find the one that is best for your story.

PICTURE BOOKS

This market covers everything produced for children from one to seven years of age in which the illustrations play a major part. Often called books for young children or K-3 (kindergarten to grade 3), they include a variety of categories.

Obviously, very small children do not buy their own books so two major groups are targeted: parents and relatives, teachers and librarians. They want durable books that entertain and educate.

Picture books include:

1. Board books and baby books are small format books, usually 16 pages, printed on paper then laminated onto board. They contain many brightly coloured illustrations and are intended for very young children.

2. Pop-up books are classified as toy books and were first produced in the 19th century. Pop-ups have inserts in the pages that become three dimensional when the book is opened. They are complicated to produce and not for the amateur.

3. Flap books are also classified as toy books and are printed on stout paper and durably bound. Illustrations contain a glued-in flap that the child lifts to reveal a picture or word concealed underneath.

4. Foldaway. A variation of the flap book, the illustration is folded back on itself, concealing part of the picture but leaving a complete image. When opened out, the image is changed. It is usually humorous or silly.

4. No text picture books. The illustrations tell the entire story so they must be created by visually minded writers. The success of these books depends on the child having enough narrative knowledge to develop the story and detail from the pictures.

5. Minimal text picture books can be read aloud or looked at. The illustrations show actions or events that extend beyond the narrative, making it possible for the reader to know something the protagonist does not. For example, the text says Jimmy is wearing too many hats. It does not say how many, but the picture completes the text by revealing three hats piled one on top of the other.

The pictures can present a broader social context than the print relates, enabling the child to explore the world contained within the illustrations. He becomes involved in the details and begins to form conclusions.

6. Long text picture books are approximately 1000 words in length and are written for slightly older children. The small number of words used to tell the story, and the use of repetitive words and phrases, give the text a poetic feel.

7. Picture Strip compresses a lot of information and story together in spreads that use limited text. The wordless picture book is an extension of this device. These books are strictly for the professional illustrator.

WRITING THE PICTURE BOOK TEXT

Most picture books are either 24- or 32-pages long, including the title and copyright pages. (1000 words, large type, will produce a 32-page book.)

A picture book is not a short story. A short story is complete and can stand on its own without need for illustration, while a picture book cannot. The text works with the pictures to tell the story that is not meant to be read without illustrations.

The author works through the details and decides which are to be written about and which are to be told with pictures. A strong visual imagination is necessary to develop a good idea into a full story.

The best picture books are straightforward observations of some aspect of a child's life. Children exist in two real worlds: the external world of activities and events that happen to them daily, and the internal world of the thoughts and feelings they have about those events.

Picture books can focus on the external or the internal world. The internal world is difficult to illustrate so the writer must provide concrete external evidence. For example, if the theme is temper, a part of every child's life, the writer needs to state the series of events precisely. Only then can the illustrator indicate the inner feelings.

Take time to plan, and polish that good idea into a wonderful book. To be successful in this market, patience and self-discipline are necessary. Try the story in both 24- and 32-page format. Making a mock-up helps to show you where the text and illustrations do not work.

Dialogue should be limited. Too much conversation is tedious to read aloud and difficult to illustrate because there is limited action. Speech balloons, included in the illustrations, are an alternative.

If you are co-publishing overseas, consider the cultural differences. Food, housing, clothing, and customs, vary from country to country. Try to keep your work centred in areas of common understanding. If this is not possible, then full explanation of the differences must be given.

Some editors are reluctant to publish when verse is used in place of prose because it can make a story sound humorous when that was not the intention. If handled incorrectly, a serious subject seems trivial.

Using animals is a favourite way of dealing with emotions that children have but cannot describe, or for those emotions that may be too harsh to illustrate in a realistic style.

The animals take on human characteristics to work through the problems. This allows the child to identify with the struggle but he is able to do so from a safe distance.

Today, the trend is to keep animals as animals. Frequently editors include in their guidelines, no anthropomorphic animals, please! Had that been the case when Wind in the Willows was written, it would never have been published.

If you are seeking a career in children's books you must look at them, read them, and learn to understand them. It helps to be with children as much as possible. Drawing from your own childhood won't always work. Nothing lessens the impact of a book more than including out-of-date details.

The market is an active one, making it necessary for you to know what is out there. Duplicating a book that is already done will get your idea rejected.

WRITING EASY READERS

Almost every major publishing company now has a line of these books. They are illustrated but they are far from being picture books. The shape and size have the appearance of an "older" book, a planned part of the presentation.

A child who has learned to read feels very important. He is no longer a baby. These books reflect that pride, but they carry concessions to the new reader: larger type, wide spaces between the lines, fewer lines, fewer words per line, and uneven right-hand margins.

Text is often broken into chapters and some have a table of contents. Easy readers average 1000-1500 words and use a 64-page format. There is a pattern running through these books.

1. VOCABULARY AND STYLE

One reason for the great success of these books is that they do not use a controlled vocabulary. They are compelling books with absorbing content, charming design, and words that challenge the reader.

Write the story clearly and forget word lists. Keep the language rich and interesting, pay attention to the sound and quality of the words, and repeat the words that challenge the reader.

Keep the sentences grammatically uncomplicated. Avoid punctuation that protracts thoughts and ideas. Short sentences are easier for the beginning reader to understand.

The plot is uncluttered and logically developed. The resolution, caused by the protagonist, is satisfying to the reader. Children love humour so add it whenever you can—funny characters or situations.

2. DIALOGUE AND PACE

Keep the dialogue short and snappy, and the story moving. The look of dialogue on a page is important because it creates white space that gives life to the page.

Action is imperative. If your characters stand still too long, your reader loses interest. They must always be "doing something" and their behaviour should be described through dialogue and activity.

3. ACTION

A good rule for new writers is to create a single action or an emotional idea in every sentence. Let the illustrations and the dialogue carry part of the action.

Where moral problems are concerned, write with honesty and directness. Keep in mind the cultural assumptions about childhood and treat differences with respect. There are certain situations that are associated with childhood: sociability, adult-marked boundaries, freedom, and fantasy. Learn to move comfortably within these conditions.

WRITING FOR JUVENILES

Juvenile fiction is designed for children eight to twelve years old and ranges in length from 2000 to 10,000 words. The story must be action-filled but not gory or horrifying. The characters can be captured or threatened as long as the description is kept within the bounds of common sense.

The story opens with the action, immediately introduces the main character and his relationship with others, and sets the scene and the mood. The plot should include a surprise kept from the reader. The use of suspense and the interaction of human emotions are two properties of skilfully constructed juvenile fiction.

Children read for pleasure, not because the book is a best seller, or because others are talking about it, or because it was a present. If a child doesn't like a book, chances are, he doesn't finish it.

Stories begin with a strong character and meaningful action, and are vivid enough to capture the reader's attention. The writing throughout must be action-orientated to keep the attention and all stories end in a satisfying manner. None should be overloaded with "preaching" disguised as storytelling, but each should contain its own inner truth.

To create the magic that keeps a child turning the pages, first find a story that gives the reader an interesting setting to expand his horizons. Taking the child to many foreign and exciting places meets this criterion but remember, your backyard can be foreign and exciting to the child with limited experience.

Setting is not simply the background against which the story is played out but the very stuff of the story itself. The characters do not determine the setting, but the setting does determine how the characters will act and what will happen to them.

Choosing the main character is the next step in developing your story. Children want to identify with the protagonist and follow his adventures to the last page.

Well-rounded characters are as necessary in juvenile fiction as they are in adult fiction. These characters are about 12-13 years old, the upper end of the age scale, and have minor faults to which the children can relate. Maybe they procrastinate or act without thinking. Maybe they are strong-willed with tempers that flare. The one thing they always are is active.

The protagonist must also have character traits that the reader can admire. Perhaps he has handled a personal problem extremely well, or has learned something that is passed on to the reader.

The story is told from the protagonist's point-of-view. Everything that happens to him is known. What the reader sees, he sees through the protagonist's eyes.

Dialogue is a significant part of juvenile fiction because it breaks up the narrative and draws the reader into the story. Mixing dialogue with fast-paced action usually results in a story the child can't put down.

The ending should always be logical and never depend on coincidence. The planning of the story should include a resolution that comes about because of the actions and reactions of the protagonist.

Once a first draft is written, it is a good idea to read it aloud to children. As you read, you will hear the bumps in the narrative rhythm, the hesitations in the dialogue, and the passages that are long and tedious.

Children are brutal critics. They don't even have to say a word—you know if you've lost them. The younger the child, the more certain you are of having a candid reaction. Should this be negative, ask your audience what they liked and didn't like. Listen to their suggestions and start rewriting.

Humour is a good ingredient in any type of juvenile fiction. Tension should not be sustained from beginning to end. Natural humour provides a breathing space.

CHAPTER THIRTEEN

YOUNG ADULT FICTION

Writing Young Adult fiction with an authentic voice requires the author to view the world as an adult and as a child. This age group, thirteen to nineteen years, is a difficult audience. Writing for them involves an understanding of the rapidly changing stages of development.

Peer pressure is more important now than at any other time. Think back to your own adolescence. Remember your first date? The first time you fell in love and the pain when, three weeks later, that love was over? Remember your friends' reactions to the major events in your life?

Now, examine these feelings and memories from your adult perspective. Emotions do not change from generation to generation. Nor do many "first" experiences, but outer trappings—clothes, fads, teenage slang—does.

What about slang? Watch for outdated expressions. Using phraseology that was popular in your youth will alert your readers, and the editor, to the fact that you are not paying attention to current trends. Language changes quickly so the idioms you hear today will likely be gone by the time your story is published. Use slang cautiously, and then only to add colour.

PLOT

The differences between story and plot, plot and theme, often confuse new writers. Look at it this way:

The husband and wife are dead. That is a simple story.

The husband is dead and the wife died of grief. That is a plot—a situation, event, or series of events. If you cannot write down a one sentence description of your story, you are going to have plot problems.

The theme of the story is the point you wish to make. Here, the theme is that the death of a loved one can be so painful that the result is disaster.

The plot should be clear in your mind before you begin to write. A story can be full of interesting characters and move along at a good pace without having a plot. When this happens, you receive editorial comment about realistic dialogue and great characters but the manuscript is rejected because the editor has no idea what the story is about.

The best way to stay on track is to write an outline. Know the characters and the problems they are going to solve. Your plot is your plan of action, the way you are going to move from beginning to end. It answers the question, "What am I writing about?"

Young Adult fiction presents its own unique set of problems. It becomes your job to find out what those interests are. The plot must be convincing, with the problems always solved by the main character. You cannot use obvious devices to get yourself out of the difficulties you've created. These readers will not accept ordinary events solved in a way that stretches credibility.

The BACKGROUND reflects the style and family history of the characters. This can be handled by mentioning tradition, religion, and place of birth. It is where they live now, the way they talk, and their education and attitudes.

If you are going to write about a race car driver, a great deal of research is necessary if you are going to be believed. Even fantasy must be done in a way that centres it in the familiar. Find a way to take your reader into that world and keep him there throughout the story.

Combining commonplace details, of life as we know it, with comparable details in the fantasy world, helps to do this. Transportation is a good example. In the future we may be flying by jet-pack instead of driving a car, but it is still transportation and can be written about in a authoritative voice.

The rules for BEGINNING, MIDDLE, and END apply. Grab your reader with the action, sustain the action, and make the ending satisfying. Young people are often "author readers." You want to build a loyal following, so you'd better leave your audience wanting more.

THEME

Fiction relies heavily on personal experience. Occasionally writers use it as a way to reach people. They believe that while the reader is being entertained, he can also be warned, persuaded or educated. It takes a very talented writer to make that work so it's wise to avoid "message" stories.

Every story has a theme, the writer's topic, that lets his personal point of view come through. Keep the points subtle and appropriate to the age of the reader. Moral courage is popular because teenagers constantly struggle with ideals and values. The stories should be perceptive of, and sensitive to, the changes in a teenager's life while offering insights into coping with problems that arise.

ACTION

Young readers wants stories packed with action. Action is movement, a sense of something happening. The older the reader, the more he can enjoy brisk dialogue, abstract ideas, character development and plot twists. However, you still can't stray too far from the action.

Sometimes the lack of action can be traced to telling the reader what is happening instead of showing him. New writers are often faced with the editorial comment, show—don't tell. They would love to . . . but how?

TELLING: Little Red Riding Hood was taking her basket filled with goodies to Grandma's house. As she walked along the path she met a wolf who asked her where she was going. Little Red Riding Hood told him she was going to Grandma's

House. The wolf got there before she did and climbed into Grandma's bed to wait for her.

SHOWING: "I must take this basket to Grandma," Little Red Riding Hood said as she filled it with cookies and fruit. "Grandma is sick and she will be happy to see me."

Little Red Riding Hood skipped along the path through the woods, singing as she went. Suddenly, the wolf jumped out from behind a tree.

"What have you got in the basket? Where are you going?" the wolf asked.

Little Red Riding Hood shook with fright. "I-I am going to my Grandmother's house," she stammered.

.....and so on.

When you show your reader what is happening, you involve him in the action.

There is no real story unless there is conflict. If Red Riding Hood hadn't met the wolf, there would be no story. She could have skipped down the path and she would have arrived at Grandma's house with a basket of goodies, but there would be no story.

CHARACTERIZATION

The beginning author should use no more than four characters in a full length story. Characters without real purpose cause confusion and dilute reader interest.

Your aim is fully developed, living characters. Writing a biography for each lets you know them inside and out. Live with your people before you write about them, and only when they become real to you should you put pen to paper.

Show your reader each character's faults and virtues; his failures and successes. Let the reader understand the character's motivation so that he understands what makes him behave the way he does.

Develop a character that provokes feelings in you and your reader will identify with all his hopes and dreams.

VIEWPOINT

Viewpoint (point-of-view or voice) is a difficult concept for many new writers. Young adult stories are often written in first person: I was perfectly happy until I stumbled upon the truth . . . It is personal, giving the reader a feeling that he knows the narrator.

With first person you write the way people speak so it is difficult to avoid slang. You are also limited because you cannot escape the narrator's opinion. The world is seen through his eyes only. You are unable to describe something even a short distance away.

You must stay "inside" your character at all times. That becomes increasingly difficult as the

story advances and the action intensifies. There are advantages in removing yourself from the character to observe him or to "report" on an activity that is happening away from him. In first person, you cannot do that.

Third person narrative: The tears began to fall. Carrie had been perfectly happy until she'd stumbled upon the truth. The author can see more of what is going on and can position himself wherever it is necessary to move the story along.

You not only know what the main character thinks and feels, but you also know what others think and feel. You can move back and forth between the characters and give insights into the story development from many different angles.

Writers often choose the third person voice while maintaining a single viewpoint. It is less personal than first person because you are not "inside" the narrator at all times, but you write everything from the single perspective.

DIALOGUE

In young adult fiction, dialogue should always have a point. When the characters speak (what they say and how they say it) they share with the reader background, emotion, or reaction that would otherwise be difficult to explain.

Dialogue helps keep the story moving. You can show a developing mystery or a budding romance through conversation. Motivation can be explained, and feelings explored.

As a writer, you must develop an ear for speech so that it can be put on paper without losing the quality that makes it real. Listen to the conversations of young people and the way they speak to their peers, their parents and teachers.

Good dialogue is not speech as it would be recorded on tape. If you wrote words as they really are, your work would be filled with slang and idioms. It would be punctuated with expressions such as gonna, yeah, and the shortcuts we all take when we speak. It would be boring and hard to read.

Reality comes from using a few expressions that show age, education, gender, excitement, fear, etc. Avoid tag words like sneered, growled, shouted. A character speaks—he says. Words are not growled, laughed, or sneered.

Review the following points.

1. The typical YA reader is 12-15 years of age.

2. The subjects are more liberal today. Stories are written about almost anything of interest to young people.

3. A YA novel is about 60,000 words in length. Stories can be any length up to 10,000 words.

4. There is a general pattern of construction but not a "formula." A character the reader likes reaches an important goal by overcoming obstacles.

5. The characters have traits with which your reader can identify.

6. Dialogue changes when teens are speaking to other teens, to parents, teachers, and so on.

FINDING IDEAS

Reading is most important when you are looking for ideas for juvenile or young adult fiction. Everything you read develops your imagination and awareness.

Some ideas originate with your own family. The changes in your children, their questions, problems and solutions, are grist for the mill. The children of friends and relatives can also supply you with ideas.

Television and movies influence the way young people act and react. Watch children at play and listen to their conversations. There is no end to a child's imagination once it is stimulated.

Ask children questions. Their answers will supply you with material and bring back incidents in your own childhood. Your subconscious is full of stories—draw from them.

Keep an Ideas Book of observations, news items, and characters that have sparked your imagination. Jot down dialogue from conversations you've overheard.

Ideas are everywhere. Once you get used to seeing them, you will never run short of things to write.

MARKETS

Writing for juvenile and young adults is not for everyone but for those who can do it, there are bonuses. This fiction has a much longer life than its adult counterparts. It is often picked up by book clubs or made into television specials.

There are youth magazines that specialize in serializing novels, as well as publishing short fiction. Writers' market material carries details for submission. Each genre, Western, Mystery, Romance, etc. has its own guidelines. When you find a market that interests you, write to the publisher and request a copy.

Potential markets include book publishers, young people's magazines, religious papers, story papers, and parenting newsletters. Payment for magazine submission is either by the word or at a flat rate, varying with length.

Books get the standard royalty. In heavily illustrated books, the royalty is split between the writer and the author. Usually, this is fifty-fifty but, with limited text picture books, the split may be sixty-forty in favour of the illustrator.

Occasionally, the illustrator will receive a larger advance from a book publisher than does the writer. The reason for this is that the editor knows the artist must purchase supplies to produce the storyboards that accompany the submission. In a heavily illustrated book, these materials can be expensive while there is little actual expense incurred by the writer.

CHAPTER FOURTEEN

THE BUSINESS END OF WRITING

Submission format is basically the same for all forms of fiction. The manuscript is typed, double spaced on 8 1/2" X 11" 20 lb. bond. The copy is clean, with no typing or spelling errors. It has a 1 1/2" margin on all sides except the first and subsequent chapter pages, which begin one third to one half down the page.

Each page is numbered and carries the name of the author and/or the title. The pages are loose—no paper clips, staples, or binding—and shipped in a box if there are more than fifty pages. A cover page, with the author's name, address, telephone/fax numbers, the type of work, the rights granted and the number of words, is included.

A brief covering letter introduces the author and the work. The letter should be no more than two pages long, perfectly typed with no spelling or grammatical errors. Remember, you are making a first impression. Publishing credits and tear sheets (samples of your work) are included in the package, along with a self addressed stamped envelope (SASE).

A query letter is not necessary when submitting short fiction, but a query letter and sample pages are required for book length fiction. Read the editorial guidelines put out by the publishers.

More publishers are asking for hard copy (printed pages) and computer disk. New markets that publish entirely on disk are surfacing. These are intended for sale to schools and libraries, are read on computers, and could be the wave of the future.

If the editorial guidelines tell you not to send unsolicited material, then don't. It won't be read. Initially, look for the houses that are open to beginners or ones that accept unagented material. DON'T PHONE THE EDITOR and try to pitch your story. The best you can hope for is a semi-polite rejection.

Once the manuscript is in the mail, forget it and start working on something else. If you haven't heard anything in two months, write a note politely requesting an update. If you haven't had an answer in four-six months, depending on the market, then you can phone the editor.

It is a good idea to enclose a reply card as well as the SASE. This is a post card, stamped and addressed to you, which says the manuscript arrived. The editor can drop it in the mail or add a note if he wants. For example: You manuscript arrived safely. Expect a reply in 2-3 months.

Always include a SASE large enough for your material to be returned if you want it back. If you have it on your computer and you don't want to spend the return postage, tell the editor to drop you a note, in the enclosed, business-size, SASE, and to destroy the manuscript.

Submitting to an international market can present a return postage problem. International Reply Coupons are available at postal outlets but they are expensive. If you have a friend living outside the country who can mail you sheets of stamps, or if you travel and can stock up, then that's the way to go.

Always state the rights you are granting to the publisher. Magazine submissions should be First North American Serial Rights or One Time Rights only. If you sell All Rights, and your story is picked up by a television station, you will receive no more money than the initial payment . . . the rights belong to the publisher and so does the money the manuscript generates.

The same applies to reprint rights and data bank submission. If a story is reprinted, you should receive more money. Make it clear that your material is not available for reprint, or use in data banks, without your permission and further payment, to be negotiated.

Simultaneous submissions will be argued for as long as there are writers and publishers. One school of thought says, send it everywhere—don't waste time. The other side argues one place at one time. I agree with one publisher at a time. If an editor takes the time and the trouble to evaluate my submission, then I should be patient enough to give him a chance to make a decision.

Should time drag on without reply, and requests for status have been ignored, then write a letter withdrawing the manuscript and submit it to the next publisher. If you insist on making simultaneous submissions, then tell the publisher you are doing so. A few don't mind, as long as they know. Personally, I don't think an editor will work as hard if he knows everyone in the country is reading the same stuff.

Pay attention to the business end of your writing. KEEP ACCURATE RECORDS. Start the day you decide to write. Initially, you can keep track of your submissions in a simple notebook or with a card file but, eventually, you will need a complete filing system.

I cross-reference with a card file and file folders stored in a cabinet. The day a manuscript is sent out, I enter the date, the editor, and the publishing house on one card bearing the manuscript name and also on another one with the publisher's name. The accompanying letters, etc., are placed in the publisher's file in the cabinet.

As correspondence arrives, notes are entered on the cards and letters placed in the file. I also have dated computer backup but I don't refer to it very often. Usually, when I need to find submission status, etc., I am working in a programme I don't want to exit to read a file.

Accurate records are imperative where the income tax department is concerned. You are largely on an honour system—and you'd better play it straight. Audits are brutal! Keep everything that pertains to your writing.

Most magazine publishers send cheques with no contracts or covering letters. It is up to you to enter your income and to keep a copy of the deposit with the name of the article written on it.

Expenses must be covered by a receipt or a statement and cancelled cheque, to be accepted by the tax department. Tax deduction laws favour the writer so take a few minutes and learn what is allowed. In many cases, losses can be written off against other income. A phone call to the tax department will give you the guidelines and an accountant may well be worth the cost.

Writing is a rewarding profession—rewarding far beyond monetary gains. You create exciting worlds and interesting people, live in places you can only dream about, climb mountains, freefall from planes, and dive to the bottom of the sea.

Writing is an exhausting profession, but it is also one of the most stimulating. It is a roller coaster of emotion as you learn to cope with rejection and acceptance. It is a constant struggle for balance.

One thing I know for sure—if you are a writer, you have to write. If you don't, you are miserable. Without writing, life is not complete.

Enjoy!